MERGER MOVEMENTS IN
AMERICAN INDUSTRY, 1895-1956

NATIONAL BUREAU OF ECONOMIC RESEARCH
NUMBER 66, GENERAL SERIES

Merger Movements
in American Industry
1895–1956

RALPH L. NELSON

NORTHWESTERN UNIVERSITY

REPRINTED WITH THE PERMISSION OF

NATIONAL BUREAU OF ECONOMIC RESEARCH, NEW YORK

UNIVERSITY MICROFILMS, INC.

A SUBSIDIARY OF XEROX CORPORATION

ANN ARBOR, MICHIGAN

1966

A STUDY BY THE

NATIONAL BUREAU OF ECONOMIC RESEARCH, NEW YORK

————◆•◆•◆————

PUBLISHED BY

PRINCETON UNIVERSITY PRESS, PRINCETON

1959

Printed in the United States of America

Foreword

The first compilation of a comprehensive and continuous series on mergers of industrial and mining corporations in the United States —no other nation has such a record—was made at the National Bureau of Economic Research exactly thirty years ago. Willard L. Thorp was its author, in his distinguished essay in *Recent Economic Changes* (1929). The series covered the years from 1919 to 1928, and a broad industrial classification was also given. This series was subsequently extended by Thorp and is now compiled by the Federal Trade Commission.

A few studies of the great wave of mergers at the beginning of the century are also available, but they are incomplete and virtually unclassified, and the period from 1904 to 1919 has been a dark age. Ralph Nelson's new series covers the entire period from 1895 through 1920, and provides more complete information on the industry, size, and type of merger than is possessed even for the recent past. The new series represents much resourceful investigation and careful verification, and students of both economic history and industrial organization will be permanently in his debt.

Not content with providing a definitive record of the most important merger movement in our history, Nelson has also tested some of the leading explanations for the tidal wave of mergers from 1898 to 1920. Three of these hypotheses—emphasizing the retardation of industrial growth at that time, the sharpening of competition consequent on development of a national transportation system, and the growth of the securities markets—receive special attention. There is also fascinating material on a host of other problems ranging from the influence of stock market levels on mergers to evidence bearing on the common belief that the original section seven (anti-merger section) of the Clayton Act ignored acquisitions of assets because they were so uncommon.

Two other National Bureau studies in industrial organization which are under way may be commented upon here. Michael Gort will soon complete a study of diversification of products by large manufacturing corporations, including both an intensive analysis of their product structure in 1954 and of its development since 1929. Light on this important and relatively modern development

—wide diversification was apparently less important before 1929, and certainly less commonly achieved by merger—will be a valuable complement of Nelson's work.

The other study is concerned with the amounts of capital and the rates of return on capital in manufacturing. Despite the strategic role of rates of return in a private enterprise economy, as both a guide to investment and a reward for efficiency, the paucity of data on this aspect of business enterprise long sheltered the subject from statistical examination. Here too we are in effect supplementing a pioneering National Bureau inquiry: Ralph C. Epstein's *Industrial Profits in the United States* (1934) was the most comprehensive study of profit rates up to that time.

Where Epstein was limited to a non-representative sample of some 2,000 large and 1,000 small corporations, it is now possible to use the corporate tax return data, which cover more than nine-tenths of manufacturing output, in essentially comparable industry detail for the period beginning with 1938. A record of capital and rates of return has been built up for a fifteen-year period, and I am now analyzing the effects of rates of return on investment, of wage rates on the substitution of capital for labor, and similar problems.

I have not mentioned numerous other National Bureau publications in industrial organization, such as *Cost Behavior and Price Policy* (1943), prepared by a committee of the Price Conference of which Edward Mason was chairman, the Universities–National Bureau Committee for Economic Research conference volume *Business Concentration and Price Policy* (1955), and Gideon Rosenbluth's *Concentration in Canadian Manufacturing Industries* (1957). They represent an important part of the literature of the subject, but I hope I will be pardoned for closing, not on a note of pride or complacency, but rather on one of hope: that there will be much more work of this kind—establishing the main contours of a remarkable economy of which we still know all too little, and examining untested hypotheses of which we have too many.

GEORGE J. STIGLER

Acknowledgment

This study, begun as a doctoral dissertation at Columbia University, was finished at the National Bureau of Economic Research, which supported the work as part of its general research program. I am deeply grateful for the assistance so generously provided.

I am especially indebted to George J. Stigler, under whom the study was begun at Columbia and through whose efforts its was continued at the National Bureau. He gave his time generously to the improvement of the work and to the education of its author. His suggestions, always constructive, encouraging, and provocative, had enormous influence in improving the study in all its aspects.

The advice and criticism of a number of others is acknowledged with appreciation. The members of the staff reading committee, Michael Gort and G. Warren Nutter, were responsible for improvements ranging over the whole work. Solomon Fabricant had much to offer in improving the first chapter, while Geoffrey H. Moore and Sophie Sakowitz were responsible for important improvements in the chapter on mergers and business cycles. The manuscript received a very thorough reading from Willard L. Thorp, a National Bureau Director by appointment of the American Economic Association. His penetrating comments, covering every part of the study, have added much to its precision and consistency. John S. Dydo of Vassar College made many constructive suggestions.

The assistance of Victor Zarnowitz, a congenial and helpful officemate, is reflected in many places. Arthur d'Antonio was a careful and thorough research assistant. The style and presentation were improved at different stages by the editorial assistance of Mary Phelps, Margaret T. Edgar, and John Sibley, and the craftsmanship of H. Irving Forman may be noted in the charts.

I conclude with a note of personal appreciation to my wife, Ann, who was a continual source of encouragement and strength in ways too subtle to describe. To all of these people, and many others, I offer my sincere thanks.

RALPH L. NELSON

Contents

CONTENTS

Tables

APPENDIX TABLES

Charts

MERGER MOVEMENTS IN
AMERICAN INDUSTRY, 1895–1956

Chapter 1. Introduction and Summary

A merger is the combination into a single economic enterprise of two or more previously independent enterprises. Mergers are surely as old as social history, and indeed many were effected through marriage. However, mergers leading to enterprises of large size relative to national markets have become significant only since the Civil War. This process had to await the development of refinements necessary to a complex industrial system, and especially to the elaboration of the business corporation. The corporation, the basic instrument for mobilizing large amounts of capital with limited liability of the investors, and essential to the development of these large enterprises, has become important in the manufacturing and mining industries only in the last seventy-five years.

The role of mergers in the evolution of our economic structure and especially of the large and often dominant industrial enterprises, has fascinated American economists and legislators since the 1890's. Unfortunately, both economic analysis and legislative policy have been handicapped by inadequate knowledge. A basic purpose of the present study is to fill the biggest gap in our knowledge, the precise extent and characteristics of mergers in the period from 1895 to 1920.

CHART I
Annual Firm Disappearances by Merger, 1895–1956

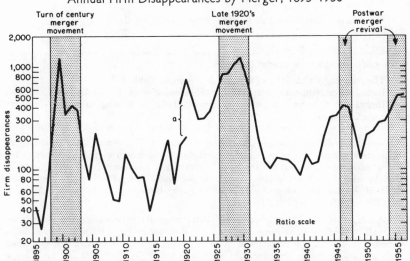

ᵃ The two series on merger disappearances are not directly comparable, and no attempt was made to splice them. A statistical comparison of the series is presented in Chapter 2.

Source: See the footnotes to Table 4.

3

An outstanding characteristic of mergers, which have been a basic force in molding our industrial structure, is the highly episodic nature of their occurrence. In three periods—1898–1902, 1926–1930, and 1946–1956—merger movements occurred on so extensive a scale that they constituted giant waves, as shown in Chart 1. This tendency of a fundamental form of expansion of industrial enterprise to show vast and widely separated peaks of activity poses a series of questions about the causes and motivations underlying mergers—questions that have interested students more, probably, than those relating to individual mergers.

One way of evaluating the importance of mergers in the growth of industrial enterprises is to pinpoint their occurrence in the history of the largest manufacturing corporations. Of the 100 largest in 1955 more than three-fifths had at least one important merger at some time in the company's history,[1] as shown in Table 1.

TABLE 1

Distribution of the 100 Largest Manufacturing Corporations of 1955
by Date of Most Important Merger[a]

Corporations having important mergers:		
Before 1895[b]	11	
1895–1904[c]	20	
1905–1915	7	
1915–1924	5	
1925–1934	11	
1935–1944	0	
1945–1955	9	63
Corporations having no important mergers:[d]		37
		100

Size of corporations measured by assets.

[a] The companies and dates of mergers are listed in Table C-1.
[b] Includes 8 oil companies created by the 1911 dissolution of the Standard Oil Company.
[c] Includes 3 cigarette companies created by the 1911 dissolution of the American Tobacco Company.
[d] Includes 2 distilling companies founded after the repeal of prohibition in 1935.

Source: *The Fortune Magazine Directory of 500 Largest U.S. Industrial Corporations*, July 1956; data compiled in present study; basic data Supplement to J. Fred Weston, *The Role of Mergers in the Growth of Large Firms*, University of California Press, 1953; Gertrude G. Schroeder, *The Growth of Major Steel Companies, 1900–1950*, Johns Hopkins Press, 1953; A. D. H. Kaplan, *Big Enterprise in a Competitive System*, Brookings, 1954; Moody's Manuals for 1929, 1939, and 1955.

[1] A merger was considered important if (1) it represented the consolidation of a number of small or medium-sized companies into one firm occupying a leading position in its industry, or (2) a leading large firm acquired another large firm, thus markedly increasing both its absolute size and its leadership in the industry, or (3) a firm acquired a number of firms—large or small—in succession, thus rapidly increasing its size and its position in the industry. The classification was necessarily arbitrary in some cases; but preferably erring on the side of rejecting mergers of uncertain importance. For example, the early Alcoa

The historical data on these largest manufacturing corporations conforms with the previously noted behavior of mergers; the important ones occurred mainly during the three major waves of the merger movement. The decade spanning the wave at the turn of the century shows the largest number (twenty), and the decade spanning the wave of the late twenties shows the second largest number (eleven).[2] The third largest number of foundation-laying mergers (nine) came in the decade following World War II; in eight of these nine corporations the mergers occurred either in 1953, 1954, or 1955.

The Three Merger Movements

The first recorded merger movement of major proportions occurred as the United States entered the twentieth century, its peak years being 1898 through 1902. In many respects it was the most important of the major merger waves. It transformed many industries, formerly characterized by many small and medium-sized firms, into those in which one or a few very large enterprises occupied leading positions. It laid the foundation for the industrial structure that has characterized most of American industry in the twentieth century.

The second large movement took place in the years 1926 through 1930. It reflected to some degree the emergence of new leading industries in the years since the first merger wave. To some degree it represented attempts to restore the industrial concentration achieved by the first merger wave, a concentration which had become diluted over the years.

The third movement, a product of the decade following World War II, differs from the two earlier merger waves, having a lower peak and a wider spread across most of the postwar decade. The five years of its highest activity were 1946, 1947, and 1954, 1955, and 1956. It was thus not so clearly a sharp burst of business reorganization as were the two earlier movements, whose greatest

(then Pittsburgh Reduction) mergers, which brought in all the crucial aluminum-making patents, were not classified as important on the ground that the acquired companies were really only patent holders, and not important aluminum producers. On the other hand, the early Westinghouse mergers, by which producing facilities were acquired, were not classified as important on the ground that the critical factors in the company's future growth were the inventions of George Westinghouse, not the producing facilities acquired through merger.

[2] The pre-1895 period also laid the groundwork for eleven of the 100 largest 1955 corporations. But of these, eight were created by the dissolution of the Standard Oil Company and were initially the result of the merger activities of only one company.

activity was bunched in five successive years. Both in the absolute volume of merger activity and in its size relative to the business population, this latest merger wave is clearly smaller than the first two. Nor is it clear that the latest merger movement has had comparable effects upon the level of concentration.

Summary of Findings

The principal empirical contribution of this study is a comprehensive and detailed series of merger activity in manufacturing and mining for the twenty-six-year period 1895 through 1920 (Chapter 3). This period was examined for two reasons. First, the huge merger wave of 1898–1902, the most important of all American merger movements, had never been adequately measured. While descriptive treatments of prominent mergers are numerous, and while penetrating analyses of their causes have been made, there existed no comprehensive statistics on the early merger movement as a whole. Second, the period of low merger activity following the peak at the turn of the century and lasting until the revival of merger activity in the 1920's had never been examined. This hitherto missing chapter in merger history completes a list of comprehensive merger series dating from 1895 through 1956. This six-decade period spans all three of the major merger movements and all but one of the minor flurries of merger activity. The only known burst of activity outside this period occurred in 1888–1892.

The data for the turn-of-the-century merger wave were used to test several of the major theories of its causes (Chapter 4). The tests permit several inferences about the nature of these causes. Empirical investigations of such factors as the rate of industrial growth, the rise of technological innovation, and the growth of interregional transportation indicated that they were not likely to have been important immediate factors in the merger wave. The leading factors of immediate importance appeared to be the newly-achieved development of a broad and strong capital market, and the existence of institutions which enabled the organizers of mergers to utilize this market. The generally favorable condition of business and a rising, buoyant securities market made practicable larger and larger units of business enterprise. This in turn permitted the centralization, in one corporate structure, of control of a large part of an industry, and made possible a more effective rationalization of industry output by business leaders. A cursory examination of the merger experience in Great Britain, where a large merger wave also occurred at the turn of the century (see Appendix A), lends positive support to this interpretation of the merger wave in the United States.

The behavior of merger activity over the sixty-two-year period 1895–1956 was examined as it related to business cycles (Chapter 5). Along with the 1895–1920 merger series compiled in this work, the series of Willard H. Thorp and the Federal Trade Commission were drawn upon for more recent years. For comparisons of mergers and business conditions the techniques developed by the National Bureau of Economic Research were used. Of the twelve clear cycles found in merger activity, eleven showed a definite timing relationship to fluctuations in general business activity (reference cycles). The few reference cycles to which mergers did not respond were among the shortest or mildest (or both) of the sixty-two-year period.

Comparison of the timing of the merger cycle with cycles in other specific economic series permitted identification of those elements in a general business cycle that might be most directly related to merger activity. Peaks in the expansion of merger activity were found to be closest in timing to those in industrial stock prices, stock market trading, and new business incorporations. Merger peaks were found to lead by a substantial interval the peaks in industrial production and the reference cycle.

It appeared that merger expansion was not only a phenomenon of prosperity, but that it was also closely related to the state of the capital market. Two reference cycle expansions, unaccompanied by a strong upswing in stock prices, were marked by the absence of a merger revival. In one instance there was a contraction of merger activity coincident with a contraction in stock prices at a time of general expansion in economic activity.

To supplement the turning point comparisons, statistical correlation tests were made of the effects on merger activity of changes in the level of industrial production and stock prices. The findings confirm those of the business cycle comparisons; the condition of the capital market, as reflected in stock price changes, has clearly been a more important immediate influence in merger activity than underlying industrial conditions have been.

The general reader is advised to proceed to Chapter 3, which presents a detailed picture of early merger activity, or to the interpretive Chapters 4 and 5. He may wish to consult Chapter 2, containing discussions of research methodology, after reading the later chapters.

Chapter 2. Scope and Methods of the Study

Industrial Sectors Studied

Merger activity will be examined only for the manufacturing and mining sectors of the economy. The study was undertaken to learn more about the merger boom at the turn of the century, and it was found, as anticipated, to have been dominated by manufacturing and mining. A concentrated investigation of these two areas was selected as more promising than an attempt to cover all sectors, in some of which (services, for example) results might be inconclusive or unimportant anyway.

An equally important reason for limiting the study to the manufacturing and mining industries was availability of data. Much of the information on mergers was obtained from financial newspapers and other business reporting services. Aside from the transportation, public utilities, and finance industries, the only ones for which information was at all adequately reported were manufacturing and mining. This was probably because the average firm size in those industries was larger than in the trades, services, construction, and agriculture. It is likely, too, that relatively more of the companies in manufacturing and mining achieved national importance. Another factor may be the greater prevalence of the corporate form of organization in manufacturing and mining. Incorporation required periodic reporting of information.

Previous Merger Series

In only a small minority of merger studies have comprehensive time series of merger activity been compiled.[1] The purpose of this study is to augment these comprehensive series in two ways, as reflected in Table 2. First, it represents an examination of the large turn-of-the-century merger wave more complete than those of existing studies, which contain serious deficiencies. Second, it bridges the gap in comprehensive merger series between 1904 and 1919. Up to now the pattern of merger activity in this period has been a mystery.

Of the four lists that were available for study of the first large merger movement, two end in the middle of the huge 1898–1902

[1] For a detailed description and survey of merger literature see: Jesse Markham, "Survey of the Evidence and Findings on Mergers," in *Business Concentration and Price Policy*, Princeton University Press for National Bureau of Economic Research, Special Conference series No. 5, 1955, pp. 141–182.

TABLE 2

Comparison of Comprehensive Time Series of Mergers in Manufacturing and Mining

Compiler	Period Covered	Time Unit	Measure of Mergers by Number of—	Measure of Size of Mergers by—	Industrial Breakdown
Bureau of Census	Pre-1887 to mid-1900	Q (de-rived)	Consolidations	Capitalization of consolidations	13 broad categories
Conant	Pre-1887 to 1900	A	Consolidations	Capitalization of consolidations	None
Moody	Pre-1887 to 1903	A	Consolidations	Capitalization of consolidations	None
Watkins	1890 to 1904	A	Consolidations	Capitalization of consolidations	None
Nelson	1895 to 1920	A & Q	Consolidations, firm disappearances by consolidation, and firm disappearances by acquisition	Capitalization of consolidations, estimated capitalization of acquisitions	Two-digit SIC categories
Thorp	1919 to 1939	A & Q	Consolidations, firm disappearances by consolidation, and firm disappearances by acquisition	No size data	10 broad categories, 1919–1928; none, 1929–1939
Federal Trade Commission	1940 to 1954	A & Q	Firm disappearances (those by consolidation and by acquisition not segregated)	Detailed breakdowns by size of acquiring and acquired firms	Two-digit SIC categories

A=annual; Q=quarterly.

For the various series, see:

Twelfth Census of the United States, 1900, Bureau of the Census, Volume VII, Part 1, pp. xxv ff.

Luther Conant, "Industrial Consolidations in the United States," *Publications of the American Statistical Association, 1901.*

John Moody, *The Truth About the Trusts,* Moody, 1904, pp. 453–469.

Myron Watkins, *Industrial Combinations and Public Policy,* Houghton Mifflin 1927, pp. 317–324.

Willard L. Thorp, in *Recent Economic Changes in the United States,* National Bureau of Economic Research, Volume 1, 1929, pp. 181–187; and "The Merger Movement," in *The Structure of Industry,* Temporary National Economic Committee, Monograph No. 27, 1941, Part III, pp. 231–234.

For 1940–1947, *The Merger Movement, A Summary Report,* Federal Trade Commission, 1948; for 1948–1954, *Report on Corporate Acquisitions and Mergers,* Federal Trade Commission, 1955. The quarterly series for 1948–1954 may be derived from the list of mergers compiled by the FTC and presented in the *Interim Report of the Antitrust Subcommittee* (No. 5), 1955, of the House Committee on the Judiciary, 84th Cong., 1st sess., pursuant to H. Res. 22 on corporate and bank mergers.

9

wave—Conant's at the end of 1900, and the Census Bureau's in mid-1900. Comparison of the four compilations on a name-by-name basis revealed considerable differences, attributable in part to the different time periods covered: Conant's from pre-1887 through 1900; Moody's from pre-1887 through 1903, Watkins's from 1890 through 1904; and the Census Bureau's from pre-1887 through mid-1900.

Comparison of the four series made for the years common to all showed differences in the number of consolidations listed. In Table 3, for the period 1890 through 1900, it will be seen that the lists

TABLE 3

Comparison of Four Merger Series for 1890–1900

Consolidations Common to—	Number of Consolidations		Percentage of Total	
Four lists:				
Moody, Conant, Watkins, and Census		62		18.7
Three lists:				
Moody, Conant, and Watkins	16		4.8	
Moody, Conant, and Census	23		6.9	
Moody, Watkins, and Census	3		0.9	
Conant, Watkins, and Census	26	68	7.8	20.4
Two lists:				
Moody and Conant	5		1.5	
Moody and Watkins	5		1.5	
Moody and Census	3		0.9	
Conant and Watkins	27		8.1	
Conant and Census	13		3.9	
Watkins and Census	3	56	0.9	16.8
One list:				
Moody	48		14.5	
Conant	37		11.2	
Watkins	24		7.2	
Census	37	146	11.2	44.1
Total		332		100.0

were more different than they were similar. Of the 332 consolidations listed for the period, 202 consolidations, or 61 per cent of the total, were found on only one or two of the lists; while 130, or 39 per cent, were found on three or on all four of the lists. Only 62 were common to all four lists, whereas 146 appeared on only one list.

ADMISSION CRITERIA

The differences result in part from the different modes of constructing the lists. Each compiler made his own rules governing inclusion and exclusion. The criteria for inclusion in each of the lists are shown in Table 4.

TABLE 4

Admission Criteria of Four Lists of Merger Activity

Criterion	Moody	Conant	Watkins	Census
Minimum size of consolidation	$1,000,000	$1,000,000	$1,000,000	No apparent limit
Authorized or issued capital	Issued	Authorized	Authorized	Not relevant
Capital types required	Equity and debt	Equity	Equity and debt	Not relevant
Geographical areas included	Local and National	Local and National	National	Local and National
Legal forms included	Wide variety	Wide variety	Wide variety	Narrow definition

The Moody list, moreover, differed markedly from the others in not being presented as a time series. It listed all the consolidations in alphabetical order and with dates given by the year in which the latest incorporation of each company took place. Thus the date might refer to a true consolidation of independent firms, a consolidation of already controlled corporations into a tighter corporate structure,[2] or simply a reorganization for some other reason.[3] Thereby, also, it excluded from mention all previous consolidations that had entered into subsequent consolidations.[4] This last bias in the Moody list has two effects. First, it understates the number of mergers over any extended period of years. Second, it produces an apparent time lag. This pattern is demonstrated in Table 5, comparing Moody's series with Watkins's. Of the two, the Moody series has a larger percentage of its consolidations in the later years of the 1890–1903 period.

ERRORS AND OMISSIONS IN THE EARLIER LISTS

In explaining differences among the four lists, the factor of accuracy in reporting is probably more important than the criteria

[2] For example, Consolidated Tobacco, incorporated in 1901 and listed by Moody for that year, was not a true consolidation. It merely replaced a loose community of interest controlling various tobacco companies by a holding company.

[3] For example, General Asphalt, listed for 1903. This was the reorganization, with no new acquisitions, of National Asphalt which was a 1900 incorporation succeeding the Asphalt Company of America, an 1899 consolidation.

[4] For example, Moody lists U.S. Steel for 1901. He does not list the previous consolidations of American Steel and Wire (1898), National Tube (1899), Federal Steel (1900), etc., all of which were consolidated into U.S. Steel in 1901.

11

TABLE 5

Mining and Manufacturing Consolidations, 1890–1903,
as Compiled by Moody and Watkins

Year	Moody		Watkins	
	Number	Percentage of total	Number	Percentage of total
1890	2	0.71	11	4.80
1891	7	2.49	13	5.68
1892	7	2.49	12	5.24
1893	7	2.49	5	2.18
1894	3	1.06	0	0.00
1895	6	2.13	3	1.31
1896	5	1.77	3	1.31
1897	5	1.77	6	2.62
1898	12	4.26	18	7.86
1899	74	26.24	78	34.06
1900	27	9.57	23	10.04
1901	46	16.31	23	10.05
1902	63	22.33	26	11.35
1903	18	6.38	8	3.50
	282	100.00	229	100.00
1890–1893		8.18		17.90
1894–1898		10.99		13.10
1899–1903		80.83		69.00

Detail may not add to totals because of rounding.

just discussed. All four overstated the number of consolidations, to a degree varying among lists and with different years. The chief cause of overstatement was the inclusion of projected but never consummated consolidations.[5] Another cause was the inclusion of nonmanufacturing and nonmining mergers in the lists.[6] A third cause of overstatement was the inclusion of both an original consolidation and its subsequent reincorporation, with no further acquisitions, in a later year.[7]

[5] For example, Watkins lists Federal Sewer Pipe as an 1899 consolidation. This proposed merger was never consummated, and many of the companies involved were consolidated in 1900 as American Clay Manufacturing. He also lists American Vinegar as an 1899 consolidation, but early in 1900 the *Chronicle* commented that it was "now counted as one of the dead projects of the year."

[6] Great Lakes Towing, for instance, listed by Moody, Conant, and Watkins for 1899, is a transportation company; United Gas Improvement, listed by Watkins in 1895, is a public utility; Consolidated Lake Superior, listed by Moody in 1897 and Conant in 1899, is a consolidation of three power companies and of one steel company. The bonds of the steel company were underwritten by the Ontario government.

[7] For example, Conant listed for 1895 American Spirits Manufacturing, incorporated that year. This was merely a reorganization of Distilling and Cattle Feeding, a consolidation of distilleries, incorporated in 1891 and listed by Conant for that year also.

In addition to these shortcomings, the four lists lacked completeness in the description of other dimensions of the merger movement. They enumerated consolidations only, without the names or numbers of firms disappearing into these consolidations. As to time units, only the Census list gave the dates of consolidation more precisely than by year of occurrence. Classifications by industry were not undertaken, nor were classifications by geographical location or by type of market.

To list only consolidations meant that the important practice of merger-by-acquisition was excluded, with very few exceptions. While it is true that the simultaneous consolidation of a number of firms into one company was the most common form of merger in this period, there were some important exceptions. The acquisition, one at a time, of independent firms over an extended period of time was characteristic of several important industries, notably the tobacco, meat packing, and gunpowder and explosives industries. The four lists lumped all this activity, if mentioned at all, at the date of a formal incorporation or consolidation, and hence to some extent distorted the true time pattern of the merger movement.

The New List

In view of the demonstrated differences among the four existing lists, and their errors and inadequacies, it was felt that an independent list should be assembled, which could serve as a check on the four and as a source for mergers possibly omitted in them. The fifth list contains both consolidations and acquisitions, and includes consolidations whose size was less than $1 million.[8]

The new list covers the period from 1895 through 1920. The research was originally planned to deal with the period from 1903 through 1920, that is, the period following the large wave of mergers between 1897 and 1903. As the inadequacies of the data on the large wave became apparent, a more complete re-examination of the period of intense activity seemed necessary. The year 1895 was chosen as the starting point because it was a time of low merger activity between the smaller 1887–1893 wave and the larger 1897–1903 wave of mergers.

The principal source of data for the new list was the weekly *Commercial and Financial Chronicle*.[9] All items on mergers from

[8] The $1 million lower cut-off limit, used in three of the existing lists was considered ambiguous for reasons discussed later in this chapter.

[9] Moody, Conant, and Watkins used this source also. I decided to use the same source to test the apparently too uncritical acceptance of it as completely reliable.

the investment news pages of this paper from 1895 through 1920 were recorded, and supplemented by information from special government reports on the steel, tobacco, and meat packing industries.[10] The new list and the four existing lists of mergers consolidated into one were used to compile a verified list of mergers.

VERIFICATION

Every consolidation was verified by a standardized follow-up procedure. The subsequent record of the firm was obtained by checking its activities as reported in the *Chronicle* and by reference to Moody's Manual, and Poor's Manual, so far as available for the year of the consolidation and the four following years. In this way one could determine with some confidence whether a consolidation had in fact been consummated, and had continued for a definite period of time. One could also usually obtain indications whether the merging firms had been independent or whether control had been in effect before the merger. This process of verification, alone, was clearly inadequate. The financial reporting services, for industrial companies at least, were in their infancy during most of the period covered. The first Moody's Manual was published in 1900, the first Thomas's Register in 1905–1906, and the first Poor's Register in 1910. Some of the consolidations were closely held corporations which would appear in the news columns only once, at the time of consolidation. Their absence from later financial news reports signified only that the business was keeping its affairs private, and not that the consolidation had not been consummated. Moreover, company name changes were not always reported by the financial news services. Therefore, news reports for the period immediately after the merger must be searched to discover name changes and dropping from public view. In the later years of the period the financial reporting services could be relied on more, as having achieved more nearly universal coverage of industrial firms.

A secondary verification procedure was therefore necessary. The companies excluded from the list in the first follow-up check were checked successively in Moody's and Poor's Manual for 1919, in the list of consolidations that Livermore[11] used in his test of the success of industrial mergers; and in the 1907–08, 1909–10, 1914,

---

[10] *Report of the Commissioner of Corporations on the Tobacco Industry*, Part I, Bureau of Corporations, 1909. *Report of the Federal Trade Commission on the Meat Packing Industry*, Federal Trade Commission, 1919. *Steel—Acquisitions, Mergers and Expansion of 12 Major Companies 1900–1950*, Hearings before the House Select Committee on Small Business, 81st Cong., 2d. sess., March 10, 1950.

[11] Shaw Livermore, "The Success of Industrial Mergers," *Quarterly Journal of Economics*, November 1935, pp. 68–96.

1921, 1923–24, and 1925–26 issues of Thomas's Register of Manufacturers. The secondary test added twenty-five consolidations to the list from among 110 excluded in the first verification procedure. Further verification attempts were believed likely to produce sharply diminishing returns.

Verification of mergers-by-acquisition was necessarily less thorough because detailed information on a year-by-year basis for subsidiary and legally merged firms was scanty. However, corroboration of a substantial fraction of acquisition disappearances was accomplished by reference to brief firm histories commonly included in the annual reports of acquiring firms listed in subsequent financial manuals. If such corroborating information was lacking, the rule was to take at face value definite statements of an acquisition in the financial news, and to reject news items phrased in the indefinite terms of rumor and prospective consummation. A substantial proportion of the acquisitions listed were in the tobacco, meat packing, steel, and explosives industries for which there was ample corroborative evidence in the form of special government reports.

DETAIL IN DESCRIPTION

One of the valuable products of this system of verification was the accumulation of detailed information about the various consolidations and acquisitions included in the recompiled list of mergers. The news items in the *Chronicle* and the brief histories and financial statements presented in the various reporting services afforded a cross-check. In this way the names and other information about acquired and acquiring firms could be checked, dates could be verified, and the real or pseudo independence of merging firms could be more clearly determined. In each merger an attempt was made to list the names of all the acquired companies. This was largely successful, but not completely so. Occasionally a consolidation would be reported as having acquired a number of companies whose names were given, accompanied by the phrase "and several more," or "and a few others," or "and many others." The word "few" was taken to mean two firms, while "several" and "many" were taken to mean three firms. There were gratifyingly few instances in which no names at all were available.

Care was used in examining lists of acquired firms to avoid counting as two or more companies those apparently under the same control. The rule was to look for identical firm names or for the reappearance, in a different title, of the same owner's name for firms located in the same city or in different cities in the same geographical region. Each consolidation represented a minor piece of detective work, and often a bit of guesswork. However, the writer thinks that, by and large, very little of such double counting got into the merger series.

A further word about the sources of data is in order. The three major sources of detailed information about the various mergers were the *Commercial and Financial Chronicle, The Truth about the Trusts,*[12] and Moody's Manual. The *Chronicle* contains in its investment news pages not only prospectuses of many projected consolidations but also the annual reports filed by those firms with the New York Stock Exchange to qualify for listing. In *The Truth about the Trusts,* Moody described the particulars of approximately 115 consolidations, and his Manual also provides a wealth of information, probably drawing heavily upon the *Chronicle.* Used in conjunction with the weekly news items about the activities of a firm under examination, these sources often contributed to rounding out the picture of a merger.

INDUSTRY CLASSIFICATION

Another product of the verification procedure was complete enough description of companies to permit detailed classification by industry. The Standard Industrial Classification system of the Bureau of the Budget, as revised in 1945 for manufacturing and 1949 for mining,[13] served as the basis of classification. More than 95 per cent of the mergers were described in sufficient detail to permit classification into three-digit categories. The main problem of classification was created by companies engaged in both manufacturing and mining. If data were sufficient, such a company was placed in the industry of its major activity; if not, the classes described in Table 6 were used. Table 6 should not be interpreted as a selection of industries in which vertical mergers were important. It refers only to those where it was not possible to determine whether manufacturing or mining was the major activity.[14]

CHRONOLOGICAL ACCURACY

One of the purposes of re-examining the early merger movement was to improve the accuracy with which the dates of the mergers

12 John Moody, *The Truth about the Trusts,* Moody, 1904.

13 *Standard Industrial Classiffication Manual* (Bureau of the Budget, Technical Committee on Industrial Classification), Vol. I, Part 1, November 1945; Vol. I, Part 2, December 1945; and Vol. II, May 1949.

14 The level of industry classification to which mergers were assigned was the three-digit level. These groupings were used as the basis for later assembly of two-digit classes. As the three-digit groups generally included relatively broad categories of industries, classification by industry usually presented no serious problem.

TABLE 6

Assignment of Industry Classes to Mixed Manufacturing and Mining Companies

Manufacturing Category		Mining Category		Classification Adopted
Activity or product	SIC number	Activity or product	SIC number	SIC number
Coke products	293	Bituminous coal	121	121
Granite products	328	Granite quarrying	141	141
Cement	324	Cement quarrying	142	142
Lime	327	Limestone quarrying	142	142
Talc refining	329	Talc mining	149	149
Iron and steel	331	Iron ore	101	331
Salt refining	289	Salt mining	147	289

were recorded, so that a more detailed time series, permitting more exact comparisons with business cycle data and other sub-annual time series data, could be presented.

The rule used in assigning dates was to record the date when control of the acquired company passed to the acquiring company, whenever this date was given. For a consolidation the date of incorporation was used if the date of transfer of control was not specifically mentioned. For a merger-by-acquisition lacking specific information, the procedure was: the month was determined by the appearance of a news item in the *Chronicle*; if the news item appeared after the tenth of the month, that month was recorded; if before the tenth day, the preceding month was recorded. This rule was waived, however, if indirect reference in the news item ("recently," or "some months ago," or a season of the year) indicated a different date of merger. Estimating the date of transfer of control was often furthered by a succession of news items describing various legal and financial actions leading to a merger, such as stockholders' meetings, the filing of applications for capitalization change, and settlement of minority shareholder suits.

These date-of-merger data, in sub-annual form, are presented as a quarterly series. A time unit as short as three months, it is believed, will do no great violence to the facts, while still permitting comparisons with other sub-annual data.

ADJUSTMENT FOR NUMBER AND SIZE OF ACQUISITIONS

The only merger-size data approaching universal availability were those of the authorized equity capitalization of consolidations. More detailed data of consolidation sizes, describing issued capitalization (either including or excluding debt), or gross assets, or sales, were found for only relatively few consolidations. Accordingly, authorized equity capitalization, though subject to many limitations, was adopted as the measuring stick of size.

In making interindustry and intertemporal comparisons of merger activity, the size of consolidations, taken alone, could be misleading, because the relative importance of mergers-by-acquisition varied between industries and between time periods. To make such comparisons more accurate, the consolidation capitalizations were adjusted by the number and size of acquisitions.

These "written-up" capitalizations are called here "merger capitalizations." Conceptually this designation comes closest to being the sum of the sizes of the merging firms. It thus includes all firms entering multifirm consolidations, where all firms are assumed to have been subordinated to the newly created corporation. It also includes firms disappearing into larger firms through direct acquisition of control. The consolidation data would be made more comparable to the acquisition data if one could deduct from the capitalization of consolidations the size of the largest firm entering each consolidation, the largest firm being assumed to have acquired all of the smaller firms. This adjustment was not possible, however, because of the lack of pre-merger size data for firms entering consolidations.

Estimates of the size of firms disappearing into mergers-by-acquisition were based on limited data collected as a by-product of the compilation and verification procedure. Frequently mention was made in the various financial news services of the gross assets, capitalization, or purchase price of such a firm. These data were used as the basis for estimating the size of acquired firms. The estimates are thus based on a mixture of measures of firm size, on the assumption that all the measures were roughly equivalent.

The series of merger capitalizations was built up as follows. The consolidation capitalization of a given three-digit product group for a given quarter-year was written up by the actual amount of the acquisition, if available. An acquisition for which no size was given was assigned a value equal to the average of the observed sizes in the product group, or, lacking more than one observation, a value equal to the average of the observed sizes for the two-digit industry of which it was a part.

The question of fluctuation of capital prices naturally arises. Available price indexes of manufacturing and mining capital indicate that capital prices fluctuated within relatively narrow limits in the period 1895–1914, and then rose rapidly in the period 1915–1920. To reduce the error that arises when prices taken from both periods are included in the average, the 1895–1914 consolidations were written up by values based upon the observed sizes of 1895–1914 acquisitions, and the 1915–1920 consolidations by values based upon 1915–1920 acquisitions. Size data were available for 464 of the 974 disappearances by acquisition in the period 1895–1914, and for 167 of the 536 acquisition disappearances of 1915–1920. The industrial representation of acquisitions with size data was quite wide for both periods, and permitted the writing up of consolidation capitalizations at the three-digit product group level in most cases.

CONSOLIDATION CAPITALIZATIONS VERSUS GROSS ASSETS

The measure of consolidation size adopted in this study was authorized equity capitalization. The vast majority of consolidations of this period—all of them until 1913—used par-value common stock. After 1913 no-par common stock became more popular; of the 133 consolidations of 1913–1920 having size data, 46 issued no-par common stock. To achieve a more exact estimate of authorized equity capitalization than that provided by authorized par-value preferred stock capitalization alone, the gross assets of the consolidation were used as the estimate of authorized capitalization.

A limited empirical test indicates that the adoption of gross assets as an approximation of "total" authorized equity capitalization probably distorts the capitalization series very little. The seventy 1895–1920 consolidations for which data on both authorized par-value common stock equity capitalization and gross assets are available show a surprisingly high degree of similarity between the two measures. Apparently there was a rough compensation process at work, with the difference between issued and authorized equity capital being roughly matched by issued debt capital. Since the balance sheets described the condition of the firm at the time of the consolidation or shortly after, the effect of earnings on the asset–capital ratio could not appear on the balance sheet at that point.

This description of the assembly of the capitalization data would be incomplete without a warning concerning their reliability. Often an asset value for a business greatly in excess of its true value was suggested by the amount of authorized (and issued) capital. Stock watering was commonplace at the turn of the century, and the popularity of such financial chicanery may have varied with the intensity of stock speculation. While it seems reasonable to expect that such manipulation might affect all industries in a roughly similar way, groups of promoters commonly being active in many industries at the same time, it is not certain that stock watering was uniform over time. Thus we cannot be sure that the capitalization series provides a wholly accurate picture of the amplitude of changes in merger activity.

If issued capitalization data had been available generally— rather than for only a few consolidations—it would have been a more accurate measure of merger size for consolidations than the authorized capitalization. While issued capital stock might be substantially watered, at least the consolidation size would not be overstated to the extent of the unissued stock. With issued capitalization for so few consolidations, it was not possible to make an appropriate adjustment of the authorized capitalization data. It is the author's impression—and it cannot be offered as anything but a very general impression—from these procedures that the turn-of-the-century consolidations usually issued all or nearly all of their authorized stock, while later ones often left a substantial part of it unissued. Greater success might be expected in times of heavy speculation than in times of more orderly market activity. If these suppositions are correct, this would have the effect of offsetting the overstatement of turn-of-the-century merger activity caused by excessive stock watering.

TOTAL VERSUS INCREMENTAL MEASURES

There are two ways of quantitatively describing merger activity, each suited to shed light on a particular set of economic problems. One expresses merger activity in terms of the total number and size of firms in which merger activity took place. The other measures it by the increase in the size of firms through merger; that is, merger activity is measured relative to the size of the to-be-merged firms at the beginning of the period under study. The most plausible rule for assigning size increases is to regard the larger of two merging firms as the acquiring firm, and the smaller of the two as the acquired firm.

For the 1895–1920 period of merger activity, a description only in terms of the first or "total" dimension is possible. The other approach must be foregone because the available data are not of sufficient detail to reveal the sizes of acquiring and acquired firms. Approximately 70 per cent of those that disappeared during the period were absorbed into multifirm consolidations, for which size data on subsidiary companies are notably sparse. Of the remaining 30 per cent that disappeared through merger-by-acquisition, more than half (58 per cent) had no size description.

20

Therefore, a measure based on the "total" dimension, or the total number and sizes of merging firms, was adopted to express merger activity.

CUT-OFF LIMIT

The reliance of this study on the financial reporting services as the source of data introduces certain sampling biases. It is quite certain that many smaller mergers escaped the attention of the financial news reporters. We are thus dealing with a relatively more complete listing of large than of smaller mergers.

To handle a sampling bias of this kind the device of the lower cut-off limit is commonly used. The function of the cut-off limit, which excludes from the list all mergers below a given size, is to give the investigator reasonable assurance that his sample represents a fairly complete list of large mergers, or at least a list permitting a reasonably satisfactory analysis of biases. This in turn permits reliable description of various dimensions of the merger movement, for mergers above the given size level. It also makes possible more reliable intertemporal comparisons of merger activity—an important consideration when the reporting procedures and biases may not be comparable for different merger studies and different periods in history.

A cut-off limit was not employed in assembling the data on mergers in this study, for two reasons. First, a cut-off limit that would attempt to omit mergers in which the acquiring (larger) firm was below a given size was precluded by the lack of data on pre-merger firm sizes. Second, no matter whether acquiring-firm size or merged-firm size were used, the predominance of simultaneous multifirm mergers in the early movement would introduce a considerable amount of ambiguity into the cut-off procedure and result in a dubious exclusion policy. For example, assuming a cut-off limit for merged-firm size of $1,000,000, the acquisition of a $350,000 firm by a $640,000 firm would be excluded, while the simultaneous consolidation of three $340,000 firms would be included. If a cut-off limit for acquiring-firm size of $500,000 were used, the three-firm merger would be excluded, and the two-firm merger would be included. In neither case does it seem desirable to include one of the mergers and not the other.

The data, when assembled, give some indication that smaller mergers were not nearly as fully reported as larger ones. There appears to be a fairly sharp drop in the number of reported mergers below certain sizes.[15] Moreover, the cut-off size shifts upward in the last six years of this period, roughly matching the rise in capital prices.[16] Whether this reflects a policy by the *Chronicle* of excluding mergers below a constant real size cannot be known. Perhaps it reflects an unstated upward revision, in the face of rising prices, in the money value of what represented a newsworthy merger.

STANDARDIZATION

In the light of the apparent large degree of underreporting of small mergers, and of a substantial rise in capital prices in the last six years of the period, certain adjustments in the data were required to make the series comparable over the whole twenty-six-year period. This was done by eliminating from the series the mergers below the points in the size scale at which the consolidations and acquisitions series "cut themselves off." Since the dollar size of the shift in the "built-in" cut-off limits between 1895–1914 and 1915–1920 roughly corresponded to the increase in the capital price level, this also had the effect of eliminating firms below the same physical size level. Thus the standardized series is at least partially free from the distortions produced by the shifting of reporting coverage and of price levels.

Consolidations less than $1,000,000 in size were eliminated in

[15] The following table shows the size distribution of reported consolidations and acquisitions for which some measure of size is given:

	Consolidations			Acquisitions	
	Average number of consolidations per $500,000 class interval			*Average number of acquisitions per $130,000 class interval*	
Size range (thousands)	*1895–1914*	*1915–1920*	*Size range* (thousands)	*1895–1914*	*1915–1920*
$ 0– 499	5	1	$ 0– 14	52	0
500– 999	17	5	15– 34	65	7
1,000– 1,499	33	5	35– 64	104	13
1,500– 1,999	22	2	65– 134	78	22
2,000– 3,499	25	6	135– 264	40	11
3,500– 6,499	16	4	265– 434	38	8
6,500–13,499	7	2	435– 564	31	8
13,500–36,499	2	0.4	565–1,164	25	7
			1,165–2,834	6	3
			2,835–4,164	3	2
Cut off point	$1,000,000	$2,000,000		$35,000	$65,000

[16] The 1919 price index of the book value of manufacturing capital was 75 per cent above its value for 1904, the mid-year of the earlier period 1899–1914; and 86 per cent above its value for 1900, the central year of the short 1898–1902 period of greatest merger activity. These figures are given by Daniel Creamer, in *Capital and Output Trends in Manufacturing Industries, 1880–1948* (National Bureau of Economic Research, Occasional Paper 41, 1954), p. 52, Chart 4.

22

the period 1895–1914, and those less than $2,000,000 in the later 1915–1920 period. Acquisitions smaller than $35,000 were removed from the 1895–1914 series, and the cut-off point for the 1915–1920 series was $65,000.

The large disparity between the cut-off limits for consolidations and acquisitions is somewhat disturbing; for both periods the cut-off limit for consolidations is about 30 times that for acquisitions. To some extent, the disparity might be expected. The acquisition data probably contain less overstatement of the real sizes of acquired firms than the data for consolidations. While much of the acquisition purchase-price data no doubt contains water, the amount of water is probably not as excessive as in the consolidation data. Also, the overstatement of consolidation size by the excess of authorized over issued capitalization was not as likely to be present in the acquisition data, in which purchase prices commonly represented the issued capital of the acquiring firm. Then, too, it could be argued that the merging activity of firms would be more likely to take the form of a consolidation if the acquired firm were large relative to the acquirer, and the form of an acquisition if the acquired firm were small. Thus we might expect to find disappearing firms systematically larger in consolidations than in acquisitions. Without dependable guides for adopting any particular ratio of consolidation to acquisition cut-off limits, it was decided to adopt those values at which the two series "cut themselves off."

Comparison of the New List with Previous Studies

The process of compilation used in this study has produced a list of mergers much more comprehensive than the four previous ones. Mergers-by-acquisition were included for the first time, and more mergers-by-consolidation than were in the other lists (see Table 7). Moreover, the additional consolidations were almost all in the above $1 million size group covered by the previous lists.

Detailed comparisons reveal that, in terms of net disappearances into mergers, the new list describes a merger wave about 27 per cent larger than the largest of the previous estimates; in terms of the adjusted capitalization of mergers, a merger wave about 20 per cent larger than the largest of the previous lists.

As the degree of understatement for number of consolidations was greater than that for capitalizations, the additional consolidations on the recompiled list are smaller, on the average, than the original consolidations taken from the old lists. This is also a

23

TABLE 7

Comparison of Number of Consolidations in the Four Previous Lists
with Number in the New List, 1895–1904

Year	New List	Census	Conant	Moody	Watkins
1895	5	2	4	2	2
1896	5	2	2	2	3
1897	10	7	4	7	6
1898	26	17	19	17	14
1899	106	74	80	79	59
1900	42 (27)ᵃ	(10)	23 (14)	25 (14)	18 (11)
1901	53			33	15
1902	48			38	17
1903	15			8	4
1904	9				1
Totals: 1895–					
Mid–1900	179	112	123	121	95
1895–1900	194		132	132	102
1895–1903	310			211	138
1895–1904	319				139

The four lists were corrected for errors and inaccuracies.
ᵃ Data in parentheses apply to the first half of 1900 only.

reflection of the disproportionate share of total capitalization accounted for by extremely large consolidations, almost fully reported on the four lists.

A relatively few very large consolidations swelled the capitalization totals. Of the total capitalization of $6.03 billion, for the 319 recompiled consolidations for 1895–1904, $2.41 billion or 40.0 per cent is accounted for by twenty-nine consolidations (9.3 per cent of the total) each with authorized capitalization of $50 million or more. Thus only one-eleventh of the consolidations accounted for two-fifths of the total capitalization. One consolidation, U.S. Steel, with a capitalization of $1.37 billion, alone accounted for 23 per cent of the total capitalization.

The recompiled list added no consolidations capitalized at $50 million or over; the main additions to the early lists were of consolidations capitalized at between $1 million and $50 million (Table 8). Comparison of consolidations capitalized at less than $1 million would be meaningless because of the cut-off limits imposed by the early compilers. The Watkins list was omitted, in Table 8, because of its exclusion of regional or local mergers, which made its understatement of the merger movement much greater than the others. The reason for the high understatement for the

TABLE 8

Ratio of Various Measures of Consolidation Activity as Recorded in
Recompiled List to Those of Early Lists

Early List	Period Covered	Size Measured by—		
		Capitalization	Net Disappearances	Number of consolidations
$50 million-and-over consolidations				
Moody	1895–1903	1.000	1.000	1.000
Conant	1895–1900	1.000	1.000	1.000
Census	1895-mid-1900	1.143	1.030	1.027
$1-to-$50 million consolidations:				
Moody	1895–1903	1.157	1.318	1.445
Conant	1895–1900	1.174	1.192	1.445
Census	1895-mid-1900	1.425	1.321	1.631

Census list as to capitalization ratio is its puzzling exclusion of the
prominent Distilling Company of America consolidation in 1899,
capitalized at $125 million.

The 1895–1920 Merger Series Compared with Subsequent Series

The comprehensive series of merger activity covering the years
following the 1895–1920 series was compiled by Willard H. Thorp
and continued after 1939 by the Federal Trade Commission (see
Table 2). For many purposes it would be desirable to splice the
two series, to provide a directly comparable, unbroken measure of
merger activity over the whole period from 1895 to the present.
Such a splicing procedure is valid only if the statistical bases for
the two series are the same or can be made the same by appropriate
adjustment. An attempt was made to evaluate the differences
between the 1895–1920 and the Thorp series to determine whether
a reliable splice might be made.

The basic sources of merger news for the two series were different: for the 1895–1920 series, the weekly *Commercial and Financial Chronicle*; for the Thorp series, the *Standard Daily Trade
Service*, first published in late 1914. The Thorp series, for the two
years of overlap, 1919 and 1920, includes about three times as many
firm disappearances as the 1895–1920 (Nelson) series (Table 9).

A name-by-name comparison of the two series could not be made
because the Thorp series does not provide this information, and
the worksheets underlying its tables have been lost. Tables 9 and
10, therefore, show the results of indirect means for comparing the
completeness of coverage of the two series. The number of firms

25

TABLE 9

Comparison of Thorp and Nelson Merger Series for 1919 and 1920

Year	Number of Consolidations			Gross Consolidation Disappearances			Acquisition Disappearances		
	Thorp	Nelson	Ratio[a]	Thorp	Nelson	Ratio[a]	Thorp	Nelson	Ratio[a]
1919	89	44	0.494	292	137	0.470	235	97	0.413
1920	173	22	0.127	474	78	0.164	459	156	0.340
1919–20	262	66	0.252	766	215	0.281	694	253	0.365

[a] Nelson to Thorp.
Source: Appendix B and Thorp, cited in Table 2.

disappearing into the "average" consolidation are presented in Table 10 for both series. The "unreported" consolidation category was derived by dividing the difference between the Thorp and Nelson gross consolidation disappearances by the difference in number of consolidations.

The two tables show that, first, the coverage of the new series relative to Thorp's declined sharply from 1919 to 1920, and second, the average size of the Thorp consolidations declined from 1919 to 1920, while Nelson's rose. Both findings are consistent with the "end effect" phenomenon. The coverage of the Nelson series would fall in the last year, as mergers accomplished in late 1920 would in some cases not be reported until 1921. (The Nelson series showed a fairly sharp decline in the last two quarters of 1920). The advance reporting in late 1918 of 1919 mergers would cause the Thorp series coverage to fall in early 1919. Smaller consolidations, usually reported only once, are especially susceptible to leads and lags in reporting. We should therefore expect the average size of Thorp's consolidations to be large in early 1919, and that of Nelson's to be large in late 1920, when, in each case, the reporting of smaller consolidations would be low.

TABLE 10

Average Gross Number of Firms Disappearing into a Consolidation, 1919 and 1920

	First Quarter 1919	Full Year 1919	Full Year 1920	Fourth Quarter 1920	1919–20
Thorp	3.67	3.28	2.74	2.64	2.92
Nelson	2.00	3.12	3.54	4.80	3.26
Thorp "unreported" by Nelson	4.50[a]	3.45	2.62	2.35	2.81

Source: Table 9 and worksheets.

For the full two-year period, the average size of Thorp's consolidations was smaller than that of Nelson's. As the number of firms entering consolidations is only a very crude measure of consolidation size, these findings must be regarded with caution. However this can be taken as at least presumptive evidence that the Nelson sample included a larger proportion of large consolidations, and that most of the additional consolidations in the Thorp series were taken from a lower stratum of the merger population.

The number of firms in both series entering the average consolidation for seven broad industry categories were compared with the proportion of establishments in central office groups and the proportion of establishments owned by corporations in 1919 (Table 11). The Nelson sample shows relatively high rank correlation between number of firms in the average consolidation and the percentage of industry establishments in central office groups; it shows low correlation between average consolidation size and percentage of establishments owned by corporations. The reverse picture was found for the Thorp sample. This finding, while not

TABLE 11

Average Number of Firms Entering a 1919–1920 Consolidation, with Percentage of Establishments in Central Office Groups and Percentage of Establishments Owned by Corporations in 1919, for Seven Industries

(ranks in parentheses)

| | Average Number of Firms Entering a Consolidation[a] | | Percentage of Establishments | |
| | | | In central office groups[b] | Owned by corporations[c] |
Industry	Thorp	Nelson		
Chemicals	4.66 (1)	3.25 (2)	19.7 (1)	86.9 (1)
Nonferrous metals	3.42 (2)	2.50 (7)	4.2 (7)	50.8 (4)
Food	2.75 (3)	3.75 (1)	7.4 (4)	27.8 (6)
Textiles	2.58 (4)	2.67 (5)	9.9 (2)	67.0 (3)
Iron and steel and products	2.49 (5)	2.84 (3)	8.0 (3)	75.4 (2)
Motor vehicles	2.45 (6)	2.57 (6)	5.0 (6)	30.3 (5)
Lumber and paper	2.23 (7)	2.75 (4)	5.1 (5)	22.1 (7)

Rank correlation between average number of firms entering a consolidation and:

	Thorp	Nelson
Percentage of establishments in central office groups	+0.357	+0.643
Percentage of establishments owned by corporations	+0.571	+0.107

a Table 10.

b Willard L. Thorp, *The Integration of Industrial Operation*, Census Monographs III, Dept. of Commerce, 1924, p. 107, Table 43.

c Derived from *Fourteenth Census of the United States, 1920*, Bureau of the Census, Vol. 10, *Manufactures, Reports of Selected Industries*.

statistically significant, is at least consistent with the evidence that the added consolidations of the Thorp sample were largely drawn from a lower stratum of the merger population.[17]

THORP AND NELSON SERIES NOT COMPARABLE

The crude comparisons presented above lend support to the assumption that the larger number of disappearances in the Thorp sample was due primarily to a more complete reporting of small mergers rather than to a more complete reporting of large mergers, though the Thorp series probably contained a somewhat more complete list of large mergers also. It seems reasonable to conclude that the 1895–1920 series includes mergers drawn largely from the upper strata of the merger population, and that it is therefore relatively free from the capricious errors that an indiscriminate mixing of merger sizes might produce.

This conclusion does not permit splicing of the two series, however. The 1895–1920 series represents a merger movement among large firms, whereas the 1919–1939 Thorp series probably represents a merger movement among large and near-large firms. As size data for 1919–1939 mergers are lacking, crude inflation of the 1895–1920 series by the ratio of firm disappearances would overstate the early merger movement. Moreover, the reporting coverage of the *Commercial and Financial Chronicle* may have undergone large changes between 1895 and 1920, a possibility we have no way of investigating. Furthermore, underlying changes in the business population, had the *Chronicle* maintained a constant reporting policy, could have caused the degree of coverage to change over time.

There is some reason to believe that turn-of-the-century merger activity was more fully reported than that of some two decades later. The leading form of merger at the turn of the century was the consolidation of many small and medium-sized firms into one

---

[17] The percentage of establishments in central office groups is not perfectly correlated with the percentage of establishments owned by corporations. Therefore, the additional Thorp consolidations could have been drawn from a lower stratum of the merger population in which the representation of central office groups was much lower, and yet one in which the representation of corporate enterprise was still quite large. The broadened merger coverage of Thorp would thus tend to produce a higher correlation with corporate ownership and a lower correlation with central office group control. One would expect some correlation between the large merger and central office group data as a large merger is more likely to result in the creation of a new central office group. This correlation probably affects our comparisons only slightly, however, as the central office statistics represent accumulated totals over many years while mergers represent additions over only two years.

28

big one; 75 per cent of 1895–1904 firm disappearances took place by the consolidation of five or more firms. In the later years of our period, 1915–1920, only 14 per cent of firm disappearances occurred through such consolidation. The many-firm consolidation was more likely to be publicly noted than the merger of only two or three small firms. As a consequence, many small firm disappearances that would otherwise not have gained public attention were probably included in the early series by virtue of the importance of the many-firm merger.[18] Other developments from the turn of the century until 1919–1920 may also have caused a shift in merger news coverage. The direction of shift is by no means clear, however. The rise in the corporate form of organization may have caused a greater coverage in the later period, since corporation news tends to be more fully reported than that of unincorporated business. On the other hand, the corporate form of organization facilitates merging; hence, in the earlier period, when fewer businesses were incorporated, a smaller part of the business population may have actually participated in mergers, and coverage may have been better than later.

In the light of these considerations, no serious attempt was made to splice the two series. Had it been done, the number of firms disappearing in the five peak years of turn-of-the-century merger activity, 1898–1902, would have been written-up by a factor of 3.2. The 2,653 disappearances would have been raised to over 8,400. The number for the five peak merger years of the late twenties, 1926–1930, was 4,838, and that for the five highest post-World War II years 2,068. By these crude comparisons the turn-of-the-century merger wave was in absolute numbers approximately 1.75 times as large as that of the 1920's; and 4.2 times as large as that of the highest postwar years.

The above comparisons, while valueless for purposes of precise description, do provide a rough idea of the importance of the turn-of-the-century merger wave, which—even after a generous allowance for overstatement—ranks in absolute size with that of the late 1920's. Set against the background of an economic system decades younger and much smaller, its importance relative to later movements becomes even more apparent.

[18] Set against this is the difference between the two series in the coverage of the principal source. The 1919–1955 series employed the daily reporting service of the Standard Statistics Company, and the 1895–1920 series employed the weekly news columns of the *Commercial and Financial Chronicle*. Had the Standard Statistics service existed before 1914 it is likely that its daily coverage of merger news would have been larger than the weekly coverage of the *Chronicle*.

Coverage of Iron and Steel Mergers in the New List

An independent test of the coverage of mergers in the iron and steel industry—one of the few for which reasonably complete independent data are available—was made for a further indication of the stratum in the merger population covered in the news columns of the *Commercial and Financial Chronicle*. The list assembled from the *Chronicle* was compared with lists in the *Directory of the Iron and Steel Works of the United States and Canada,* published by the American Iron and Steel Institute.[19] Before 1916 the *Directory* was in the process of developing its lists toward the more complete coverage of later editions. Accordingly, two comparisons were made, one for the period before 1908, and one for 1916–1920.

COVERAGE BEFORE 1908

The 1908 *Directory*, with listings as of November 1907, contains (Part I) complete data for 101 companies, including corporate structure, officers, details of number, size, and type of iron and steel works, and merger activities. A second listing (Part II) contains all iron and steel works, including those owned by the 101 companies (Part I) along with the others. The data in the second part are extremely sparse, apart from description of the size and type of works, and it was not possible to determine whether mergers had occurred among the firms listed there. Thus the comparison of coverage was carried out with the 101 companies—a substantial proportion of the iron and steel industry, as is shown in Table 12.

TABLE 12

Share of Iron and Steel Industry Equipment Owned by 101 Firms, 1907

	Amount		
	101 Firms	Industry	Percentage
Number of blast furnaces	275	448	61.5
Number of steel works and rolling mills	215	598	36.0
Blast furnace capacity[a]	27,071	34,834	77.8
Steel ingot capacity[a]	27,868	34,140	81.8

a Thousands of gross tons.

Source: *Directory of Iron and Steel Works of the United States and Canada,* American Iron and Steel Association, Seventeenth Edition, 1908, Preface and Part I.

[19] Before 1913, the American Iron and Steel Association. See Seventeenth Edition, 1908; 1910 and 1912 Supplements to the Seventeenth Edition; Eighteenth Edition, 1916; and Nineteenth Edition, 1920.

30

From the table it is safe to infer that all of the major steel companies are represented in the list of 101. It contains ten of the twelve largest steel companies later described by Schroeder,[20] the missing two being Sharon Steel (organized in 1900 and still very small in 1907) and National Steel (not organized until 1929).

Of the 101 firms 30 were subsidiary companies, and one was listed twice in the index, leaving 70 independent iron and steel companies in the *Directory* list, 20 of which exhibited no merger activity in this period. In the fifty mergers there were 441 (gross) disappearances of firms, of which 17 were not found on the list compiled from the *Chronicle*. Thus, for those firms for which the independent check was possible there is a coverage of 96.2 per cent in this study.

Of the 50 companies in which mergers occurred 10 were not principally in the iron and steel industry (S.I.C. 33), but as classified in the compilation were either in the fabricated metal products (34), machinery (35), or transportation equipment (37) industries. However, most of them did own blast furnaces or rolling mill facilities, or both, and thus were included in the *Directory*. If these are excluded from the comparison the gross number of disappearances is reduced to 385. Since no disappearances into these 10 companies were among those omitted from the recompiled list, the number of omissions remains 17, and the completeness of coverage in that list for companies engaged primarily in the production of basic iron and steel products is thus 95.6 per cent.

COVERAGE FROM 1916 THROUGH 1920

By 1916 the *Directory* provided detailed data as submitted by all the iron and steel companies listed alphabetically by name. By comparing the 1920 and 1916 listings in the *Directory*, it was possible to compile a list of mergers which could be taken as complete. Capitalization and capacity data for many acquired firms were also given, which permitted a separate comparison of the coverage for large and small acquisitions. The *Directory* reports 81 acquisitions in the period 1916–1920;[21] for 54 of them the size of the acquisition as measured by capacity is given, and for 44 the size measured by capitalization. Of the 81 acquisitions found in the two editions of the *Directory*, 40 were also found in the

---

[20] Gertrude G. Schroeder, *The Growth of Major Steel Companies, 1900–1950*, Johns Hopkins Press, 1953.

[21] The eighty-one acquisitions taken from the directory were exclusively iron and steel companies, and did not include machinery producers, transportation equipment makers, and other fabricators having blast furnace and rolling mill facilities.

Chronicle, among which 29 had capacity data and 25 had capitalization data.

The completeness of coverage for large and small acquisitions is summarized in Table 13. The *Directory* listed 18 acquisitions

TABLE 13

Coverage of Large and Small Iron and Steel Company Acquisitions, 1916–1920

Size of Acquisition	Number Listed in Iron and Steel Directory (1)	Number in Col. 1 also listed in Chronicle (2)
Capitalization:		
$1,000,000 and over	18	17
Less than $1,000,000	26	8
Size not given	37	15
	81	40
Capacity:ᵃ		
70,000 tons and over	16	16
Under 70,000 tons	38	13
Size not given	27	11
	81	40

ᵃ Capacity data in tons of pig iron, or steel ingots, or both.

Source: American Iron and Steel Institute, directories for 1920 and 1916, cited in text footnote 19; and worksheets.

capitalized at $1 million and over, 17 of which were mentioned in the *Chronicle.* The coverage of acquisitions of less than $1 million capitalization was much lower, with the *Chronicle* mentioning only 8 of the 26 found in the *Directory.* For those having no size data, presumably small firms, the *Chronicle* coverage was also small. The average capacity of a $1 million firm appeared to be about 70,000 tons, with considerable variation among firms. Use of that figure as a size boundary indicates much the same pattern of coverage as shown by the capitalizations data.

Chapter 3. The Merger Movement from 1895 through 1920

The large wave of mergers at the turn of the century has never been characterized in sufficient detail to permit definitive analysis; no earlier discussions covered such important aspects as industry composition, size distribution, and type of merger. The merger pattern from 1904 to 1919 has never been described at all. The study makes possible a survey of this dimly perceived yet important quarter-century of merger history. The immense merger peak of 1899–1901 will be more clearly revealed, and it becomes more impressive when set against the mergers of the two succeeding decades.

After a survey of the fluctuations in merger activity, later sections will deal with its industrial composition and size distribution, the comparative roles of acquisitions and consolidations, and the distribution of merger activity among states, that is, by state of incorporation. As throughout, observation is confined to the manufacturing and mining industries.

CHART 2

Quarterly Series of Firm Disappearances by Merger, Unsmoothed, 1895–1920

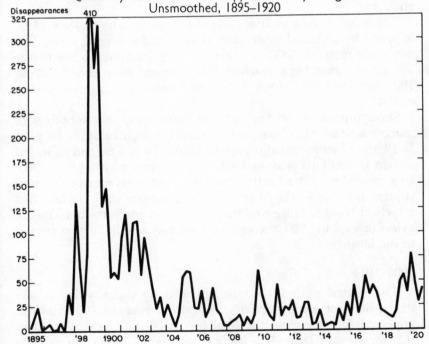

Source: Table B-2

The Time Pattern

Chart 2 presents the quarterly series of firm disappearances by merger from 1898 through 1920. It suggests a division into three subperiods, each characterized by the predominant nature of its merger activity:

Subperiod	Description
1895–1904	Turn-of-the-century merger wave
1905–1914	Decade of low merger activity
1915–1920	Expansion of merger activity

Patterns of change during the several periods appear as follows.

1895–1904

In this ten-year period the average number of firms disappearing annually was 301. Five of these years, 1898–1902, saw a burst of merger activity never exceeded in importance in our history, with 1,028 firms disappearing into mergers in 1899 alone. The huge turn-of-the-century merger wave produced U.S. Steel, American Tobacco, International Harvester, Du Pont, Corn Products, Anaconda Copper, and American Smelting and Refining, to name only a few. Its effect on American industry was widespread and enduring.

There had been a smaller cycle of merger activity in 1888–1893, followed by a virtual suspension of mergers for several years. The new cycle began in 1895 at a level of merger activity so low that it has never again been reached. The merger wave ebbed during 1903 and 1904, and reached its lowest point in the third quarter of 1904.

Superimposed upon the ten-year wave were two subcycles of merger activity. The first had its initial trough in 1896, its peak in 1899, and its terminal trough in 1900. The second had its initial trough in 1900, its peak in 1901, and its terminal trough in 1904. In a sense the reduced activity of 1900 represents merely an interruption midway in the huge 1898–1902 merger wave, rather than a cyclical trough. Since underlying series in production and stock prices dipped in 1900, the interruption may also be in part related to the business cycle.

1905–1914

The second period was distinguished by the absence of any strong burst of merger activity. A yearly average of 100 firms disappeared into mergers, the total for the decade being less than that for the year 1899. This is not to say that no important mergers occurred between 1905 and 1914, a period which saw the formation of General Motors in 1908, Computing-Tabulating-Recording (later International Business Machines) in 1911, and Aetna Explosives in 1914. Nevertheless, general merger activity was at a low ebb; in only one year (1905) did firm disappearances into mergers reach more than 150.

Two cycles are observed in this period of low merger activity. The first had its initial trough in 1904, its peak in 1905, and its terminal trough in 1908; the second had its initial trough in 1908, its peak in 1910, and its terminal trough in 1914. In both, the expansion interval was shorter than the contraction interval, inviting the interpretation of this period as an extension of the declining phase of the huge turn-of-the-century merger wave. However, the variety of legal and economic factors responsible for the sharp contraction of merger activity from 1902 to 1904 strongly suggests that the period following 1904 was fundamentally different from the huge turn-of-the-century merger wave.

1915–1920

In this six-year period firms disappeared into mergers at an average rate of 139 per year, much lower than the 301 yearly average of 1895–1904, but well over the 100 yearly average of 1905–1914. It is probably fair to describe this as the initial phase of the higher merger activity that was to characterize the 1920's. By 1917 the number of firm disappearances by merger had reached 195, a level equal to that of 1919 and 1920, and not exceeded since 1905.

This period also saw the first recurrence of the very large consolidation since the early merger wave of 1898–1902. After the U.S. Steel consolidation of April 1901 there was none larger than $136.5 million until 1917 when the $283 million Union Carbide and Carbon consolidation was formed. This was followed in 1919 by the $198 million Transcontinental Oil consolidation, and in 1920 by the $283 million Allied Chemical and Dye consolidation.

The series of cycles in merger activity continued in the third subperiod. In this short span (six years), only one full cycle was observed, with its initial trough in 1914, its peak in 1917, and its terminal trough in 1918. The expansion interval was longer than the contraction, suggesting that the cycle may have been superimposed on a general upswing of merger activity. The suggestion is strengthened by contrast with the reverse expansion-contraction interval patterns observed in the three preceding merger cycles of 1900–1904, 1904–1908, and 1908–1914, all of which were superimposed on either a general downswing or a sustained period of low merger activity.

FIRM DISAPPEARANCES AND MERGER CAPITALIZATIONS

The magnitude of merger activity can be described in two ways: first, in terms of the net number of firms disappearing because of merger, i.e. the net reduction in the business population due to mergers;[1] second, in terms of the sum of the sizes of firms disappearing into mergers. The measure of firm size used in this study is the capitalization of the mergers; hence the name *merger capitalizations*.[2]

A division of the period into subperiods on the basis of adjusted merger capitalizations gives essentially the same breakdown as that based on firm disappearances, as Table 14 shows. The only major exception is that in the third subperiod (1915–1920) the absolute level of capitalizations of the first period had been almost regained. This rise in merger capitalizations relative to disappearances was mainly due to a rise in capital prices, and not to a strongly discernible increase in the real size of firms entering mergers. Both annual series exhibit very high activity at the turn of the century, followed after 1904 by a decade of relatively low activity and, in the last six years of the period, a revival of merger activity. The two series also exhibit a high degree of conformity in their cycles of merger activity (Table 15).

These findings are probably what would be expected. With the data in annual form, relieved of the irregularities found in shorter time units, there should be relatively little divergence between the disappearances and capitalizations series. We might expect the divergence to be greater during periods of generally low merger activity, when a few large mergers might more easily dominate the capitalizations series. This may explain the divergence of the two sets of peak year dates (1905 and 1906, 1910 and 1912) during the decade of low merger activity, 1905–1914.

SPREAD OF CHANGES IN MERGER ACTIVITY AMONG INDUSTRIES

A supplementary indication of the magnitude of merger activity in any given period of time is the industrial representation of

---

[1] If, for example, ten firms enter into a consolidation, the gross number of firms disappearing is ten, but the net decrease in the business population as the result of the consolidation is nine. Adjustment for net disappearances puts all the lists on the same standard of comparison, i.e., the decline in business population resulting from the consolidations. Thus the distortion of comparisons of data containing both disappearances of old independent firms and appearances of new consolidated companies is avoided by using net data.

[2] The basic data were the authorized capitalizations of consolidations which were written up (adjusted) at the product-group and industry level by the estimated sizes of firms disappearing by acquisition. For a detailed description of this process see Chapter 2.

TABLE 14

Firm Disappearances by Merger and Merger Capitalizations, 1895–1920

Year	Firm Disappearances by Merger	Merger Capitalizations (millions of dollars)
1895	43	40.8
1896	26	24.7
1897	69	119.7
1898	303	650.6
1899	1,208	2,262.7
1900	340	442.4
1901	423	2,052.9
1902	379	910.8
1903	142	297.6
1904	79	110.5
1905	226	243.0
1906	128	377.8
1907	87	184.8
1908	50	187.6
1909	49	89.1
1910	142	257.0
1911	103	210.5
1912	82	322.4
1913	85	175.6
1914	39	159.6
1915	71	158.4
1916	117	470.0
1917	195	678.7
1918	71	254.2
1919	171	981.7
1920	206	1,088.6
AVERAGE ANNUAL MERGER ACTIVITY		
1895–1904	301.2	691.3
1905–1914	100.1	220.7
1915–1920	138.5	605.3
1895–1920	186.3	490.4

Source: Tables B-3 and B-7.

TABLE 15

Trough and Peak Years of Merger Cycles, 1895–1920

Trough Years		Peak Years	
Disappearances	Capitalizations	Disappearances	Capitalizations
1896	1896	1899	1899
1900	1900	1901	1901
1904	1904	1905	1906
1909	1909	1910	1912
1914	1914 or 1915	1917	1917
1918	1918		

Source: Table 14.

changes in its merger activity as compared with the period preceding it. If, between two successive periods of time, merger activity in a number of different industries changes in the same direction, we have a sound basis for characterizing the more active period as what is usually called a *merger movement*. If the aggregate volume of merger activity increases because of disproportionately large increases in a few industries, the characterization of the over-all change as a merger movement may be unwarranted.

The average annual merger activity of twenty-seven Standard Industrial Classification two-digit manufacturing and mining industries for the three subperiods was computed. The twenty-seven two-digit classes include twenty-one manufacturing classes and four mining classes; two additional classes defied assignment—ice, including both natural and manufactured ice production, and a heterogeneous group of industries containing elements of both manufacturing and mining.[3]

The changes in their average annual merger activity between the three subperiods 1895–1904, 1905–1914, and 1915–1920 are summarized in Table 16. Between 1895–1904 and 1905–1914 the average annual merger activity declined in twenty-four of the twenty-seven two-digit industries as measured by disappearances, and in twenty-three of them as measured by capitalizations. The decline was greater than 40 per cent in nineteen of the twenty-seven industries for disappearances and in seventeen for capitalizations. The upswing in merger activity between 1905–1914 and 1915–1920 was not nearly so widespread as the downswing between 1895–1904 and 1905–1914 had been. Hardly more than half of the twenty-seven industries—that is, fifteen or sixteen, as measured by disappearances or by capitalizations—experienced an increase in merger activity. The growth, while not widespread, was notable for the important industries which spearheaded it. Of the nine two-digit industries having an increase greater than 100 per cent in average annual merger capitalizations, six were large industries in which mergers played an important role (Table 17).

SUMMARY

The breakdown of the twenty-six-year period into three distinct parts seems justified. The three subperiods exhibit different levels of merger activity, each encompasses an integral number of cycles of merger activity, and the variations in merger activity among periods have distinct industrial compositions. The findings above tend to confirm, and to show more accurately, what has been agreed

3 For a listing of the industries, see note to Table 19.

about the time pattern of mergers in this period—that the turn-of-the-century merger wave was large and important, and that it was followed by a protracted period of low merger activity.

TABLE 16

Interperiod Changes in Average Annual Merger Activity for
Twenty-Seven Two-Digit Industry Classes, 1895–1920
(*number of industries in indicated categories of increase or decrease in firm
disappearances and merger capitalizations*)

	Disappearances	Capitalizations
BETWEEN 1895–1904 AND 1905–1914		
Increase	3	4
Decrease		
0–40%	5	6
40–80%	12	13
Over 80%	7	4
BETWEEN 1905–1914 AND 1915–1920		
Increase		
Over 100%	8	9
50–100%	4	2
0–50%	3	5
Decrease		
0–50%	5	6
50–100%	7	5

Source: Appendix B.

TABLE 17

Merger Growth from 1905–1914 to 1915–1920 of Six Leading 1915–1920
Merger Industries

Industry	Percentage Growth of Average Annual Merger Capitalizations	Rank Among 27 Industries by 1915–1920 Merger Capitalizations[a]
Petroleum products (29)	+2177.7	1
Chemicals (28)	+1271.6	2
Primary metals (33)	+104.4	3
Transportation equipment (37)	+364.7	4
Petroleum & gas extraction (13)	+919.6	7
Metal products (34)	+264.7	8

Numbers in parentheses following names of industries denote sic numbers in this and the following tables.

[a] That is, by absolute annual averages.

Source: Appendix B.

An unexpected finding is that merger activity began to recover in the years preceding the entrance of the United States into

World War I. Because the previously existing comprehensive series of mergers began no earlier than 1919, they left uncertain whether the early twenties saw the first instance of a major revival of merger activity since the turn of the century. The findings of this study place the upswing as early as 1916–1917. To the degree that this dating is correct, the second great merger movement in the United States is seen to be not strictly a creature of the "roaring twenties" but a longer-run phenomenon originating considerably earlier.

Industrial Composition

One of the features of the 1895–1920 period was the participation in mergers of virtually all of the manufacturing and mining industries. This study records mergers in all of the twenty-one two-digit manufacturing industries and in four of the five two-digit mining industries, the one exception being anthracite coal mining (11). Although there were numerous indirect indications of mergers in anthracite coal, acquisitions by certain railroads dominated the merger picture in this industry. Examination of anthracite coal mergers would, therefore, have entailed a separate study of railroads, which was outside the scope of the study. It might also be noted that the anthracite coal industry was almost the classical example of the use of the "gentlemen's agreement" in organizing an industry.[4]

Merger activity was found not only in nearly all manufacturing and mining industries for the whole twenty-six-year period, but the industrial representation was complete also for the three subperiods, with one exception, ordnance (19) in the period 1905–1915. In only nineteen of the eighty-one subperiod industry categories were fewer than ten firm disappearances recorded. The industrial composition was by no means uniform, however, some industries experiencing a very large amount of merger activity and others very little. Nor was the industrial composition constant over time. The purpose of the following section is to describe this heterogeneous and changing industrial pattern of mergers.

MANUFACTURING AND MINING

The two industry groups studied, manufacturing and mining, differed in terms of gainful workers employed and of realized private production income: manufacturing was seven to eight times as large as mining. Approximately the same proportion was

[4] On this, see Eliot Jones, *The Anthracite Coal Combination in the United States*, Harvard University Press, 1914.

found also between total merger capitalizations in manufacturing and in mining. This measure, given in Table 18, indicates that mergers played roles of roughly the same importance in both manufacturing and mining.

Within the twenty-six-year period, there were substantial changes in the relative shares of manufacturing and mining in merger activity. This pattern is also seen in Table 18. Manufactur-

TABLE 18

Distribution of 1895–1920 Merger Activity Between Manufacturing and Mining
(per cent)

	Net Firm Disappearances by Merger			Merger Capitalizations		
Period	Manufacturing	Mining	Not allocable	Manufacturing	Mining	Not allocable
1895–1920	78.9	17.4	3.7	87.6	10.7	1.8
1895–1904	81.2	15.8	3.0	90.7	7.4	2.0
1905–1914	67.3	25.3	7.4	74.1	22.5	3.5
1915–1920	84.7	13.6	1.7	89.6	9.9	0.5

Detail may not add to totals because of rounding.

ing dominated the merger activity of the first and third subperiods, accounting for four-fifths or more of firm disappearances and nine-tenths of merger capitalizations in both 1895–1904 and 1915–1920. In the middle period, 1905–1914, however, mining accounted for approximately one-fourth of merger activity, partly because of the persistence of mergers in bituminous coal after the large 1898–1902 wave. In the decade 1905–1914 the bituminous coal industry accounted for a greater number of firm disappearances into mergers than any other two-digit manufacturing or mining industry. It moved from eighth place in 1895–1904 to fourth place in 1905–1914 among the twenty-seven industries in size of merger capitalizations. The persistence of mergers in metal mining also contributed to the increasing importance of mining mergers in the 1905–1914 decade. In terms of firm disappearances, metal mining rose from fifteenth to ninth place among the twenty-seven industries between 1895–1904 and 1905–1914, and from tenth to third place in terms of merger capitalizations.

DISTRIBUTION BY INDUSTRY, AND ITS CHANGES

The distribution of 1895–1920 merger activity among the twenty-seven two-digit industries is presented in Table 19. Though merger activity was found in all twenty-seven two-digit industries,

TABLE 19

Distribution of 1895–1920 Merger Activity in Manufacturing and Mining
by Two-Digit Industry Classes

Industry	Firm Disappearances by Merger	Merger Capitalizations (millions of dollars)
Ordnance (19)	18	57.8
Food and kindred products (20)	758	1,231.1
Tobacco products (21)	180	412.9
Textiles (22)	167	403.3
Apparel (23)	5	12.0
Lumber, wood products (except 25) (24)	48	54.4
Furniture, fixtures (25)	36	26.2
Paper and allied products (26)	155	192.2
Printing, publishing (27)	18	37.9
Chemicals (28)	360	1,032.7
Petroleum products (29)	170	1,038.8
Rubber products (30)	36	162.5
Leather and products (31)	38	81.1
Stone, clay, glass products (32)	226	211.2
Primary metals (33)	634	3,852.1
Metal products (except 19, 35, 37) (34)	269	482.4
Machinery (except 36) (35)	263	638.9
Electrical machinery, etc. (36)	63	139.4
Transportation equipment (37)	270	940.8
Instruments, optical goods, etc. (38)	30	46.0
Miscellaneous manufacturing (39)	79	104.3
Metal mining (10)	111	441.2
Bituminous coal mining (12)	573	615.9
Petroleum and gas extraction (13)	99	210.5
Nonmetallic minerals mining (14)	119	95.9
Ice, natural and manufactured	122	156.9
Not allocable	57	73.1
All manufacturing (19–39)	3,823	11,167.8
All mining (10, 12–14)	842	1,363.6
Other	179	230.0
Total	4,844	12,752.4

Source: Appendix B.

The abbreviated form in which the industry classifications are given does not signify any difference in coverage from the classifications given in the SIC *Manual*. The titles given there are:

Manufacturing

19. Ordnance and accessories.
20. Food and kindred products.
21. Tobacco manufactures.
22. Textile mill products.
23. Apparel and other finished products made from fabrics and similar materials.
24. Lumber and wood products, except furniture.
25. Furniture and fixtures.
26. Paper and allied products.

42

Manufacturing (continued)

27. Printing, publishing, and allied industries.
28. Chemicals and allied products.
29. Products of petroleum and coal.
30. Rubber products.
31. Leather and leather products.
32. Stone, clay and glass products.
33. Primary metal industries.
34. Fabricated metal products, except ordnance, machinery, and transportation equipment.
35. Machinery, except electrical.
36. Electrical machinery, equipment, and supplies.
37. Transportation equipment.
38. Professional, scientific, and controlling instruments; photographic and optical goods; watches and clocks.
39. Miscellaneous manufacturing industries.

Mining

10. Metal mining.
12. Bituminous coal and lignite mining.
13. Crude petroleum and natural gas extraction.
14. Mining and quarrying of nonmetallic minerals, except fuels.

---

the great majority of merger activity occurred in eight industries: food and kindred products (20), chemical and allied products (28), petroleum products (29), primary metals (33), metal products (34), nonelectrical machinery (35), transportation equipment (37), and bituminous coal mining (12). The eight industries accounted for 68.2 per cent of 1895–1920 firm disappearances by merger and for 77.1 per cent of merger capitalizations. Among them, the first four groups—food, chemicals, petroleum products, and primary metals —accounted for 39.8 per cent of firm disappearances and for 56.1 per cent of merger capitalizations. Primary metals alone accounted for 13.1 per cent of firm disappearances and for 30.2 per cent of merger capitalizations.

Within the twenty-six-year period 1895–1920 there were numerous shifts in the share of merger activity among the twenty-seven two-digit industries. These reflected the important and complex changes in the pattern of industry in this period, particularly the over-all growth of industry, and the differential participation in this growth by individual industries.[5] For example, the output of the petroleum and coal products industry (29) grew 282 per cent between 1904 and 1919, and petroleum products ranked first in the volume of 1915–1920 merger capitalizations. The output of leather products increased only 22 per cent and leather products ranked twenty-first in 1915–1920 merger capitalizations. Also

[5] Solomon Fabricant, *The Output of Manufacturing Industries, 1899–1937*, National Bureau of Economic Research, 1940, Table 1, p. 44; Table 5, pp. 60–61.

important were the increasing average size of industrial firms, and, especially, changes in the size-distribution of firms generally and in specific industries. Between 1914 and 1919 the average number of wage earners per establishment in chemicals and allied products (28) increased 44 per cent, while that in lumber and its products (24) increased only 6.1 per cent.[6] Chemicals ranked second in 1915–1920 merger capitalizations, while lumber products ranked twenty-fourth. Probably important also, in certain industries, was previous merger activity which, by the level of concentration achieved, had effectively limited subsequent merger activity over an extended period of time. For example, the reappearance of large merger àctivity in petroleum products after the pre-1895 monopolization by the Standard Oil trust may have had to await both the substantial growth of the industry and the 1911 dissolution of the Standard Oil Company.

In view of this changing pattern of industry it is not surprising that the industrial composition of merger activity underwent a large change over this 'period. This shift is indicated in Table 20, in which the twenty-seven manufacturing and mining industries are ranked by size of merger activity for the three subperiods and for the full twenty-six-year period.

The table shows that there was probably a greater shift of ranks from 1905–1914 to 1915–1920 than from 1895–1904 to 1905–1914.[7] This finding is consistent with the hypothesis, suggested above, that changes in the composition of merger activity tend to reflect differential changes in industry growth rates. Arthur F. Burns found that the decade 1905–1915 was one of widespread retardation in growth in industry.[8] As such it was probably not a propitious time for large changes in the industrial composition of merger activity. There was a substantial increase in the number of industries showing large growth rates in the period 1915–1920, however, and this may be reflected in the somewhat greater change in the industrial composition of merger activity between 1905–1914 and 1915–1920.

[6] Willard L. Thorp, *The Integration of Industrial Operations*, Census Monograph III, 1924, Table 9, p. 41.

[7] The lower the correlation between ranks, the greater the shift in ranks between two periods. Statistical tests of the significance of the difference between correlation coefficients gave the following results: For the disappearances data, there was no significant difference between the changes of ranks from first to second periods and the changes from second to third periods. For the more meaningful capitalizations data, the difference bordered on the statistically significant. We would expect such a large difference to be due to chance in only one of twelve samples. All four rank correlation coefficients are significantly greatèr than zero at the 1 per cent level of significance.

[8] Arthur F. Burns, *Production Trends in the United States since 1870*, National Bureau of Economic Research, 1934, Table 13, p. 81; see also Table 41 in Chapter 4 below.

TABLE 20

Industrial Composition of 1895–1920 Merger Activity:
Rankings for Twenty-Seven Two-Digit Industries

Industry	Merger Capitalizations				Firm Disappearances by Merger			
	1895–1920	1895–1904	1905–1914	1915–1920	1895–1920	1895–1904	1905–1914	1915–1920
Primary metals (33)	1	1	1	3	2	2	3	4
Food and kindred products (20)	2	2	2	5	1	1	2	3
Petroleum products (29)	3	16	10	1	10	20	13	1
Chemicals (28)	4	6	8	2	4	4	5	5
Transportation equipment (37)	5	3	6	4	5	9	7	2
Machinery (except 36) (35)	6	4	5	10	7	7	4	9
Bituminous coal mining (12)	7	8	4	6	3	3	1	10
Metal products (except 19, 35, 37) (34)	8	7	11	8	6	6	10	6
Metal mining (10)	9	10	3	17	15	15	9	13
Tobacco products (21)	10	5	9	14	9	8	11	16
Textiles (22)	11	9	7	9	11	12	8	8
Petroleum and gas extraction (13)	12	19	19	7	16	16.5	15.5	7
Stone, clay, glass products (32)	13	12	22	11	8	5	19.5	12
Paper and allied products (26)	14	11	25	15	12	10	24	11
Rubber products (30)	15	14	12	16	22.5	24	15.5	18
Ice, natural and manufactured	16	13	13	19	13	14	6	17
Electrical machinery, etc. (36)	17	15	17	13	18	19	22.5	14
Miscellaneous manufacturing (39)	18	17	15	26	17	13	21	20
Nonmetallic minerals mining[a] (14)	19	22	14	18	14	11	12	19
Leather and products (31)	20	20	16	21	21	23	17.5	21
Nonallocable	21	18	20	27	19	16.5	14	22.5
Ordnance (19)	22	26	27	12	25.5	26.5	27	15
Lumber, wood products (except 25) (24)	23	21	18	24	20	18	17.5	27
Instruments, optical goods, etc. (38)	24	23	21	22	24	22	25	22.5
Printing, publishing (27)	25	25	23	20	25.5	25	19.5	25
Furniture, fixtures (25)	26	24	26	23	22.5	21	22.5	25
Apparel (23)	27	27	24	25	27	26.5	26	25

Rank correlations (Spearman) for industrial distribution of merger activity 1895–1920, between subperiods

Period Compared	Measure of Merger Activity	
	Disappearances	Capitalizations
1895–1904 and 1905–1914	+0.742	+0.825
1905–1914 and 1915–1920	+0.620	+0.587

Source: Appendix B.

The shifts among leading merger industries (Chart 3) tend to support the hypothesis. The three industries growing in merger importance after 1914—transportation equipment (mainly automobiles, trucks, and parts), chemicals, and petroleum products— were industries that experienced large rates of growth, with large increases in both the number and size of firms.

CHART 3

Shares of Total Merger Activity of Leading Merger Industries, by Subperiod, 1895–1920

Numbers in italics indicate rank of given industry in volume of merger activity among twenty-seven two-digit manufacturing and mining industries.

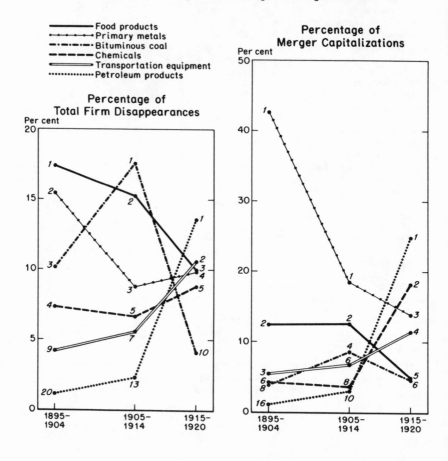

INTRAINDUSTRY PATTERNS

If changes in the composition of merger activity were examined, using finer (three-digit) levels of industry classification, there would perforce be a greater number of shifts in rank than at the two-digit level. The following brief sections summarize changes among three-digit classes for four important two-digit industries—food products, chemicals, primary metals (manufacturing and mining), and transportation equipment. This material reveals that the rise through merger of single large enterprises and changes in the product makeup of enterprises were important factors in the shifting industrial composition of merger activity at the finer levels of classification.

Food Products. The most striking shift in merger activity in the food products industry was the decline in the beverages group, shown in Table 21. Led by brewery and distillery mergers, bever-

TABLE 21

Distribution of Merger Activity among Product Groups within the
Food Products Industry, 1895–1920

| | Percentage of Merger Capitalizations | | |
Product Group	1895–1904	1905–1914	1915–1920
Meat products (201)	9	17	39
Dairy products (202)	1	2	9
Canning and preserving (203)	7	2	28
Grain mill products (204)	5	1	5
Bakery products (205)	8	25	2
Sugar (206)	13	12	9
Confectionery (207)	3	2	2
Beverages (208)	37	10	0
Miscellaneous (209)	16	30	6
	100	100	100
Average annual merger capitalizations			
(thousands of dollars)	78,229	27,643	29,562

Detail may not add to totals because of rounding.
Source: Worksheets.

ages predominated in merger activity during the first wave, and then their participation declined to only a fraction of one per cent of food products mergers in the period 1915–1920. Passage of the Eighteenth Amendment in 1919 contributed to lowering that share; but the substantial decline from 1895–1904 to 1905–1914 indicates that merger activity in beverages had begun to drop off

47

well before Prohibition. The decline was probably the result of very intensive merger activity before 1904. By 1904 Distillers Securities, successor to the Distilling Company of America, had achieved a commanding position in the liquor market, and the major problem facing the company was to integrate its far-flung empire of small and large distilleries. Its post-1904 activity seemed to revolve around attempts to sell off its small distilleries and to consolidate operations in the larger ones. It was eventually forced to sell a large Peoria distillery, and it was continually beset by new competition, which it tried to forestall through trade agreements rather than by merger.

Chemicals. The most conspicuous development in mergers of chemical firms was the emergence of the multiproduct merger in the last six years of the period 1895–1920. This appears in Table 22 in the "not elsewhere classified" category to which were assigned

TABLE 22

Distribution of Merger Activity among Product Groups within Chemicals and Allied Products, 1895–1920

	Percentage of Merger Capitalizations		
Product group	1895–1904	1905–1914	1915–1920
Industrial organic chemicals (mainly explosives) (282)	4	21	6
Paints and varnishes (285)	9	13	7
Fertilizers (287)	22	49	1
Vegetable and animal fats (288)	28	5	1
Not elsewhere classified	9	1	83
All other	28	11	2
	100	100	100
Average annual merger capitalizations (thousands of dollars)	29,294	8,018	109,912

Detail may not add to totals because of rounding.
Source: Worksheets.

mergers of firms each producing products found in different three-digit categories. It includes the very large consolidations of Union Carbide and Carbon (1917) and Allied Chemical & Dye (1920). It also includes acquisitions by Du Pont of celluloid, synthetic fabrics, and paint firms after the dissolution of the explosives company in 1911.

The consolidation form of merger played a leading role in the chemicals industry.[9] One-sixth of its total merger capitalizations of

[9] The one great exception is the pre-1911 activities of the then explosives company, DuPont, which acquired most of its competitors, one at a time, over an extended span of years.

1905–1914 was accounted for by the 1914 consolidation of several independent powder companies, former Du Pont subsidiaries, into the $12.5 million Aetna Explosives Company. A single consolidation also accounted for the increase in the share of fertilizers in chemical mergers in 1905–1914: the $24 million International Agricultural Corporation, a 1909 consolidation of nine phosphate companies, alone accounted for 30 per cent of total 1905–1914 chemical merger capitalizations. The American Linseed consolidations of 1898 accounted for about one-fifth of the chemical merger capitalizations of 1895–1904, and for about three-fourths of the total for vegetable and animal oil mergers in the same period. Table 23 shows the prominent role of consolidations in chemical mergers, in comparison to the merger movement in general.

TABLE 23

Consolidation Capitalizations as Percentage of Merger Capitalization,
Chemicals and All Manufacturing, 1895–1920

	1895–1904	1905–1914	1915–1920	1895–1920
All manufacturing	88	50	54	73
Chemicals	81	67	85	83

Primary Metals. Shifts in the relative size of merger activity between iron and steel and nonferrous metals mergers are presented in Table 24. Manufacturing and mining are combined in both industry categories to eliminate any bias in the data due to different degrees of vertical integration among firms in the two industries.[10] Nonferrous merger activity continued at a fairly high level after the large turn-of-the-century wave, while iron and steel mergers dropped off sharply. This persistence of merger activity in nonferrous metals in 1905–1914 was a major cause of the increased share of mining versus manufacturing in merger activity at that time (Table 18). Then, as merger activity in general recovered after 1914, nonferrous activity declined substantially, while iron and steel mergers staged a vigorous comeback.

[10] This bias arises from the arbitrary convention adopted for this study by which a mixed manufacturing-mining merger is assigned to the industry group apparently representing the greater amount of its activity. In the two industries discussed here the convention leads to an overstatement of iron and steel *manufacturing* mergers relative to those in nonferrous metals, and conversely to an overstatement of nonferrous *mining* mergers relative to those in iron and steel. In particular, only eight disappearances are assigned to the iron ore mining category, while ninety-nine are assigned to the nonferrous mining category. All vertical (mine plus mill) iron and steel mergers were placed in manufacturing, as the blast furnace steel mill function was judged to be the major activity; only some of the vertical nonferrous mergers were so judged.

49

TABLE 24

Relative Merger Activity in Ferrous and Nonferrous Metals Industries, 1895–1920

| | Average Annual Merger Capitalizations (thousands of dollars) | | |
Industry	1895–1904	1905–1914	1915–1920
Iron and steel (331, 332, 101)	257,234	26,324	61,687
Nonferrous (333–336, 102–106)	51,173	37,754	20,545
Ratio: iron and steel to nonferrous	5.0	0.7	3.0

Source: Appendix B and worksheets.

Transportation Equipment. The shift in transportation equipment mergers from railroad equipment to motor vehicles between 1895–1904 and 1915–1920 is clearly seen in Table 25. Railroad equipment mergers led the first decade of the twenty-six-year period, accounting for more than two-thirds of merger activity in the industry. Motor vehicles, however, played the principal role thereafter, accounting for five-sixths of the industry's mergers in the second subperiod, and for three-fourths in the third.

TABLE 25

Distribution of Merger Activity among Product Groups within Transportation Equipment, 1895–1920

| | Percentage of Merger Capitalizations | | |
Product Group	1895–1904	1905–1914	1915–1920
Motor vehicles and equipment (371)	12	85	77
Aircraft and parts (372)			3
Shipbuilding and repairing (373)	11	8	8
Railroad equipment (374)	69	7	3
Motorcycles, bicycles and parts (275)	8		
Not elsewhere classified (379)			8
	100	100	100
Average annual merger capitalizations (thousands of dollars)	37,610	14,906	70,085

Detail may not add to totals because of rounding.
Source: Worksheets.

The moderate decline indicated in the share of shipbuilding is probably inaccurate because the amount of shipbuilding merger activity is understated for the periods 1905–1914 and 1915–1920. Bethlehem Steel, under the leadership of Charles M. Schwab, was quite active in acquiring shipbuilding companies in the years before and early in World War I. These acquisitions have been assigned to the steel industry, under the rule of classifying a merger by the industry of greater activity.

RELATIVE VERSUS ABSOLUTE MERGER ACTIVITY

The above comparisons deal with absolute merger activity. For many purposes of description the absolute measure is satisfactory, but for most analytical purposes it is inadequate. For example, it is useless for examining the results of mergers in terms of the achievement of high concentration of control in an industry. A very large industry may exhibit large absolute merger activity which, nevertheless, if measured relative to the size and number of firms in the industry, may be insignificant. On the other hand a small industry, while showing only moderate absolute merger activity, may undergo a major change in concentration of control as the result of its mergers.

It has not been possible to express the size of merger activity of the various industries relative to the size of the industry with any satisfactory degree of precision. The data on industry size in the first decade of our period were notable for their paucity, probable inaccuracy, and noncomparability to the size data for mergers gathered in this study. However, an attempt was made to express 1895–1907 merger activity as a percentage of industry size in 1904 for fourteen manufacturing industries for which size data roughly comparable to the merger size data were available. Comparison of absolute and relative measures of merger activity, using capitalization as the measure of firm and industry size, is presented in Table 26. Methods used in estimating relative merger activity and for making other comparisons are presented in detail in Appendix D.

The six or seven industries leading in absolute merger activity were, with one or two exceptions, also the industries leading in relative merger activity. The ranks of the leaders vis-à-vis each other, however, underwent minor shifts between absolute and relative measures of merger activity. Nevertheless, the coefficient of rank correlation between absolute and relative measures of merger activity for the fourteen industries was sufficiently high (+ 0.736) to encourage the assumption that high absolute merger activity was roughly indicative of high relative merger activity.

A similar assumption that the absolute number of firm disappearances could be used as a rough measure of relative merger activity is unwarranted, however. In comparisons of absolute and relative measures of merger activity based on disappearances, the correlation was much lower (+ 0.363).[11] This is probably to be expected, since the average firm size varies greatly among industries. For example, the highly populated food and kindred products

[11] Table D-3.

TABLE 26

Absolute and Relative Merger Activity of Fourteen Industries
Measured by Capital, 1895–1907

| Industry | Absolute Merger Activity | | Relative Merger Activity | |
	Merger capitalizations (millions of dollars)	Rank	Percentage	Rank
Primary metals (33)	3,168.4	1	210.0	1
Food and kindred products (20)	937.8	2	39.4	9
Machinery (except 36) (35)	404.0	3	71.9	3
Transportation equipment (37)	391.0	4	75.1	2
Tobacco products (21)	314.3	5	47.6	6
Chemicals (28)	245.3	6	50.6	5
Textiles (22)	213.5	7	14.5	11
Stone, clay, glass products (32)	160.5	8	40.5	8
Paper and allied products (26)	157.4	9	56.7	4
Electrical machinery, etc. (36)	78.8	10	43.8	7
Petroleum products (29)	74.0	11	1.5	14
Leather and products (31)	45.2	12	18.6	10
Lumber, wood products (24) and furniture, fixtures (25)	42.3	13	8.2	12
Printing, publishing (27)	18.9	14	4.9	13

Source: Tables B-3 and D-1.

industry, with small average firm size, ranked first in absolute number of firm disappearances through merger, but stood twelfth out of fourteen in the relative number of disappearances. Stone, clay, and glass products, also a populous small-firm industry, ranked fourth in absolute number and ninth in relative number of disappearances.

SUMMARY

Mergers were found in all major manufacturing and mining industries, but a disproportionate share was accounted for by a relatively few industries. The eight leading merger industries were primary metals, food products, petroleum products, chemicals, transportation equipment, fabricated metal products, machinery, and bituminous coal. Together, they accounted for 77 per cent of merger capitalizations and 68 per cent of net firm disappearances by merger during the twenty-six-year period under study.

An equally important aspect of the picture was the shift among industries in their relative shares of merger activity over the years. Petroleum products and chemicals replaced primary metals and food products as leaders in merger activity. In transportation equipment, the predominant segment for merger activity during 1895–1904 was railroad equipment; during 1915–1920, motor vehicles. The greater change in the industrial composition of merger activity came between 1905–1914 and 1915–1920, rather than between 1895–1904 and 1905–1914. The post-1914 rebirth of merger activity saw not only a growth in general activity but also the emergence of new industries to lead this growth.

Size Distribution

The size distribution of 1895–1920 mergers shows a shifting pattern in which the earlier and later parts of the period are in contrast. The decade 1895–1904, containing the large turn-of-the-century merger wave, was characterized by the many-firm consolidation; the period 1915–1920 on the other hand was characterized by consolidations of few firms and by the acquisition of one firm by another. The pattern is summarized in Table 27.

TABLE 27

Distribution of Firm Disappearances by Type of Merger, 1895–1920

(*per cent*)

	1895–1904	1905–1914	1915–1920
Acquisitions and consolidations of two to four firms	25.0	62.3	86.1
Consolidations of five or more firms	75.0	37.7	13.9

CONSOLIDATIONS

Consolidations, taken alone, played a decreasingly important role in mergers from 1895 to 1920. Not only were there fewer consolidations per year in 1915–1920, but there were also fewer firms entering the average consolidation, as Table 28 shows. The median number of firm disappearances into consolidations declined from 5.2 in 1895–1904 to 2.7 in 1915–1920. The mean number of firm disappearances into consolidation declined from 9.0 to 3.5. Consolidations representing the simultaneous union of ten or more firms were 26.3 per cent of the total in 1895–1904, and in 1915–1920 only 1.4 per cent of all consolidations.

During the same time span, however, the average size of consolidations as measured by authorized capitalization declined only moderately if at all. The mean consolidation capitalization of 1895–1904 was $19.2 million, while that of 1915–1920 was $16.7 million (Table 29). The median size, however, increased from $6.3 million in 1895–1904 to $7.3 million in 1915–1920.

TABLE 28

Distribution of Consolidations by the Number of Firms Consolidating, 1895–1920

(*per cent*)

Number of Firms Consolidating	1895–1904	1905–1914	1915–1920
2	20.7	20.7	44.7
3	13.9	23.0	22.7
4	10.2	10.1	10.6
5–6	15.7	14.4	17.0
7–9	13.3	9.4	3.6
10–16	13.6	11.5	1.4
17–25	4.9	1.4	—
26–40	5.9	—	—
41	1.9	—	—
Median	5.2	3.2	2.7
Mean	9.0	4.9	3.5
Average annual number of consolidations	31.3	13.2	18.5
Consolidation disappearances as percentage of all merger disappearances	83.5	52.5	34.5

Source: Worksheets.

TABLE 29

Distribution of Consolidations by Authorized Capitalizations, 1895–1920

(*per cent*)

Authorized Capitalization[a] (millions of dollars)	1895–1904	1905–1914	1915–1920
1.0 to 1.5	8.0	7.3	4.6
1.5 to 2.5	10.6	11.4	7.3
2.5 to 3.5	11.3	10.6	11.9
3.5 to 6.5	22.9	22.0	22.9
6.5 to 13.5	18.6	30.9	29.4
13.5 to 36.5	17.3	13.8	16.5
36.5 to 63.5	6.0	3.3	3.7
63.5 to 136.5	4.7	0.8	0.9
136.5 and over	0.7	—	2.8
Median	$6.3	$6.3	$7.3
Mean	$19.2	$9.0	$16.7
Consolidation capitalizations as percentage of all merger capitalizations	87.2	53.7	52.4

Detail may not add to totals because of rounding.

[a] The frequency classes were chosen so that the most common capitalizations would fall at the mid-point of the class interval, or the several most common values would be symmetrically distributed across the class interval, or both. In most cases the authorized capitalization appeared to be a convenient round number, selected by the organizers of the enterprise, and it probably exceeded the projected amount of issued capitalization by a comfortable margin.

Source: Worksheets.

It appears from comparison of Tables 28 and 29 that, although the number of firms entering the average consolidation declined, the decline was at least partly offset by an increase in the average size of firms entering consolidations. A simple arithmetic mean computed by dividing the total consolidation capitalizations of a subperiod by the gross number of firm disappearances into consolidations bears this out. The average size of firms entering 1895–1904 consolidations was $2.1 million, that of firms entering 1905–1914 consolidations was $1.8 million, and that of 1915–1920 consolidations disappearances was $4.7 million. These shifts in average disappearance size are due mainly to the presence of a few very large consolidations and to changes in the price level of capital.

To remove the influence of the few very large consolidations from our comparisons will give a clearer picture of size changes for the majority of consolidations. Accordingly Table 30 summarizes the changes in consolidation activity after omission of five very large ones: the $200 million Federal Steel consolidation of 1898 and the $1,370 million U.S. Steel consolidation of 1901, which together accounted for 26 per cent of 1895–1904 consolidation capitalizations; and three 1915–1920 consolidations—Union Carbide and Carbon, Transcontinental Oil, and Allied Chemical and Dye—with a combined capitalization of $764 millions, or 40 per cent of the total for those years. On that basis, the average size of 1895–1904 consolidation disappearances becomes $1.6 million, that for 1905–1914, $1.8 million, and that for 1915–1920, $3.0 million.

The apparent increase in the average size of 1905–1914 consolidation disappearances over the average of 1895–1904, and the apparent further increase of 1915–1920 probably result largely from increases in the price level of capital. Because the price indexes and measures of firm size are quite crude, no strong inference about size changes over the period can be made. Clearly, however, the data do not indicate any major increase in the size of consolidation disappearances in the last six years, 1915–1920.

We may then characterize the consolidation activity of 1895–1920 as follows: Consolidations predominated in the first part of the period and played a role equal to that of acquisitions in the later years. The decline in the importance of consolidations was marked not only by a decrease in their number, but also by a reduction in the number of firms entering the average consolidation. Apart from a very few large consolidations, the average real size of firms entering consolidations in 1915–1920 was not appreciably larger than in earlier years. Thus the decline in the number

TABLE 30

Breakdown of Changes in Consolidation Activity, 1895–1920

	Percentage Change	
	1895–1904 to 1905–1914	1905–1914 to 1915–1920
Average annual consolidation capitalizations[a]	−73 (−80)	+60 (+168)
Average annual number of consolidations	−58 (−58)	+40 (+44)
Average dollar size of firms entering consolidations	+16 (−15)	+61 (+164)
Number of firms entering average consolidation	−46 (−45)	−29 (−29)
Average dollar size of firms entering consolidation	+16 (−15)	+61 (+164)
Price level of capital[b]	+14 (+17)	+48 (+48)
"Real" size of firms entering consolidation	+ 2 (−26)	+ 9 (+78)

Figures in parentheses include the five atypical very large consolidations: Federal Steel (1898), U.S. Steel (1901), Union Carbide and Carbon (1917), Transcontinental Oil (1919), and Allied Chemical and Dye (1920). These five comprised a total of $2,334 millions or 25.4 per cent of all 1895–1920 consolidation capitalizations.

[a] The percentage change in average annual consolidation capitalization is the product of the percentage changes in average annual number of consolidations, average dollar size of entering firms, and number of firms entering average consolidation, all expressed in decimal form relative to a base of one.

[b] The Creamer index of the "price" of book value of manufacturing capital was used to deflate capitalizations. The value of the index for 1900 was 94.06; for 1909, 107.27; for 1914, 113.45; and 1919, 175.21 (1904 = 100). A weighted average price index was computed for 1915–1920 by weighting annual interpolations (straight line), for 1915 to 1920 by number of firm disappearances into consolidations. Its value is 158.93.

of consolidation disappearances was not offset, in any important degree, by an increase in the size of disappearing firms.

ACQUISITIONS

The importance of acquisitions in total merger activity increased steadily from 1895 to 1920. Acquisitions accounted for 16.5 per cent of net merger disappearances in 1895–1904, 47.5 per cent in 1905–1914, and 65.5 per cent in 1915–1920. In terms of adjusted merger capitalizations the acquisition form of merger accounted for 12.8 per cent of 1895–1904 merger activity, 46.3 per cent of 1905–1914 activity, and 47.6 per cent of 1915–1920 activity. The failure of the 1915–1920 acquisition share of merger capitalizations to grow with the share of firm disappearances was due much more to the appearance of three very highly capitalized consolidations than to a decline in the size of acquisition disappearances. The size distribution of firms disappearing by acquisition is given in Table 31. Both the median and mean sizes of 1915–1920 acquisi-

TABLE 31

Size Distribution of Acquisition Disappearances, 1895–1920

Acquisition Size[a] (thousands of dollars)	Percentage of Total Number of Acquisitions Having Size Data		
	1895–1904	1905–1914	1915–1920
35 to 265	25.7	21.2	15.7
265 to 835	35.5	28.1	20.5
835 to 1,165	14.7	13.3	10.8
1,165 to 2,835	13.5	19.7	21.1
2,835 to 4,165	2.0	10.8	12.1
4,165 to 14,165	6.5	4.9	15.7
14,165 to 35,835	1.6	1.5	4.2
35,835 and over	0.4	0.5	—
Median acquisition size	$655	$830	$1,404
Mean acquisition size	$1,780	$2,150	$3,190
Number of acquisitions having size data	245	203	166
Total number of reported acquisitions	497	475	544

Detail may not add to totals because of rounding.

[a] The frequency classes were chosen so that the most common sizes would fall at the midpoint of the class interval, or the several most common values would be symmetrically distributed across the class interval, or both.

Source: Worksheets.

tions are substantially larger than those of 1895–1904 and 1905–1914. This is also seen in the proportion of acquisitions larger than $2,835 thousand. Only 10.5 per cent of 1895–1904 acquisitions were larger than $2,835 thousand, while the corresponding percentages were 17.7 for 1905–1914 and 32.0 for 1915–1920.

The greater apparent size of 1915–1920 acquisitions may be partly caused by a sampling bias. The frequency distributions of size were reported by the financial news services. The ratio of acquisitions having size data to all reported acquisitions varied presented in Table 31 are based on acquisitions for which measures over time: from 49.7 per cent in the first decade of the period to 42.7 per cent in the second, and to 30.5 per cent in the last six years. Thus the size distribution of acquisitions for 1915–1920 is based on a much smaller proportion of all reported acquisitions than those of the preceding decades.

If the acquisitions for which size data were available tended to be somewhat larger, on the average, than those having no size data, there would be an upward bias in the 1915–1920 distribution of acquisition sizes. That the bias is probably not large, however, was ascertained by the following test.

A reconstruction of the 1915–1920 distribution was carried out by adding a number of acquisitions sufficient to equalize the coverage with that of 1895–1904. They were distributed in accordance with the straight line distribution produced by plotting the 1895–1914 distribution on double logarithmic paper.[12] The median value of this reconstructed frequency distribution is $835 thousand.

When the median size for 1915–1920 from the original and reconstructed distributions is deflated by the capital price index, contradictory indications of size trend result. The original distribution would indicate that the real acquisition sizes were about 25 per cent larger in 1915–1920 than in 1895–1914, and the reconstructed distribution would indicate that they were about 25 per cent smaller. Probably the most accurate conclusion is that the data reveal no strong trend toward either larger or smaller acquisition sizes.

SUMMARY

Examination of the size distribution of merger activity suggests that changes in the relative importance of the consolidation and acquisition forms of merger over the twenty-six-year period resulted chiefly from changes in the number of firms entering a merger rather than from changes in real firm sizes over time. The apparent changes in real firm size were the effect of a very few extremely large consolidations rather than of general shifts in firm sizes.

The decline in the relative importance of the consolidation form of merger was brought about in two ways. First, the average annual number of consolidations formed declined from 31.3 in 1895–1904 to 18.5 in 1915–1920. Second, the number of firms entering the average consolidation declined also, from 9.0 in 1895–1904 to 3.5 in 1915–1920. Acquisition disappearances, on the other hand, increased from an average of 49.7 per year in 1895–1904 to 90.7 per year in 1915–1920.

The Merger Process

It is useful, for certain purposes, to distinguish between the consolidation form of merger and the acquisition form. The distinction is in part between single and multiple mergers, and in

---

[12] The 1895–1914 and 1915–1920 distributions were plotted on double logarithmic charts. The 1895–1920 distribution traced as a straight line for sizes above $265 thousand. The distribution of larger 1915–1920 acquisitions closely approximated that of larger 1895–1914 acquisitions. However, for 1915–1920 acquisitions below $2,835,000, the frequency fell progressively below those for 1895–1914. Accordingly, the 1915–1920 frequency classes below $2,835,000 were written up to the level that a straight line comparable to that for the 1895–1914 distribution would produce.

part between all-at-once and one-at-a-time mergers. A consolidation is the more or less simultaneous multiple-union of firms into a consolidated company, an acquisition is the taking over of one firm by another, either as an isolated action or as one of an extended series.

The economic and legal factors involved in an acquisition may be different from those involved in a consolidation. Consolidations may represent an attempt to secure a dominating market position directly, without a lengthy competitive war. A series of acquisitions, too, may represent attempts to secure market control, especially if legal restrictions or insufficient financial resources prevent consolidating a large number of firms at one time. On other grounds, a consolidation may represent the success of a promoter in convincing a number of firms to unite into a new, highly capitalized company. In such a case the psychological value of simultaneous action may be important in assuring the successful consummation of the merger. In times of less frenzied merger activity, therefore, we might expect a relative decline in the use of the consolidation form. Consolidation might be the more common form for mergers of large firms in which the organization of a new, more highly capitalized corporation may be necessary. Finally, and perhaps as important as any factor, changing fashions in the enactment and interpretation of the various states' corporation laws may cause changes in the form and timing of mergers.

The proportions of total merger activity accounted for by consolidations and acquisitions are presented in Table 32. Over the whole twenty-six-year period consolidations dominated merger activity. They accounted for more than two-thirds of the merger activity of the period, as measured by either capitalizations or firm disappearances. Within the period, however, there were large shifts in the relative shares of consolidations and acquisitions. Consolidations dominated the first decade of the period, accounting for seven-eighths of merger capitalizations and five-sixths of net firm disappearances by merger. In the second decade the role of acquisitions was almost equal to that of consolidations, the merger activity dividing 53–47 in favor of consolidations. In the final six years of the period, acquisitions dominated firm disappearances by merger, accounting for two-thirds of merger activity thus measured, but only for half of the merger capitalization total. The main reason for the different proportions shown by the two measures is the occurrence of three atypical very large consolidations in this period. Union Carbide and Carbon, Transcontinental

TABLE 32

Distribution of Merger Activity by Form of Merger, 1895–1920

	Merger Capitalizations			Firm Disappearances		
	Total	Percentage by—			Percentage by—	
	(millions	Consolida-	Acquisi-		Consolida-	Acquisi-
Year	of dollars)	tion	tion	Total	tion	tion
1895	40.8	84.6	15.4	43	86.1	13.9
1896	24.7	89.1	10.9	26	84.6	15.4
1897	119.7	92.4	7.6	69	89.9	10.1
1898	650.6	94.6	5.4	303	93.1	6.9
1899	2,262.7	92.1	7.9	1,208	91.7	8.3
1900	442.4	88.1	11.9	340	89.9	14.1
1901	2,052.9	92.4	7.6	423	83.2	16.8
1902	910.8	76.2	23.8	379	70.7	29.3
1903	297.6	49.5	50.5	142	39.4	60.6
1904	110.5	28.1	71.9	79	45.6	54.4
1905	243.0	43.4	56.6	226	63.7	36.3
1906	377.8	57.1	42.9	128	35.9	64.1
1907	185.8	36.6	63.4	97	50.5	49.5
1908	187.6	89.8	10.2	50	72.0	28.0
1909	89.1	40.4	59.6	49	24.5	75.5
1910	257.0	44.8	55.2	142	52.8	47.2
1911	210.5	76.7	23.3	103	67.0	33.0
1912	322.4	58.5	41.5	82	45.1	54.9
1913	175.6	37.5	62.5	85	45.9	54.1
1914	159.6	38.2	61.8	39	48.7	51.3
1915	158.4	46.3	53.7	71	42.3	57.7
1916	470.0	44.9	55.1	117	38.5	61.5
1917	678.7	59.1	40.9	195	42.1	57.9
1918	254.2	21.3	78.7	71	9.9	90.1
1919	981.7	61.9	38.1	171	43.3	56.7
1920	1,088.6	51.1	48.9	206	23.8	76.2
1895–1904	6,913.4	87.2	12.8	3,012	83.5	16.5
1905–1914	2,205.8	53.7	46.3	1,001	52.6	47.4
1915–1920	3,639.5	52.4	47.6	831	34.5	65.5
1895–1920	12,758.7	71.5	28.5	4,844	68.7	31.3

Source: Appendix B.

Oil, and Allied Chemical & Dye accounted for $764 million in capitalizations and only 9 net (12 gross) firm disappearances. If these consolidations are removed from the comparison, the share of consolidations in 1915–1920 merger capitalizations declines from 52.4 per cent to 39.7 per cent. The share of net merger disappearances declines from 34.5 to 33.9 per cent. Thus, excluding the very large consolidations, acquisitions are seen to have played the dominant role in 1915–1920 merger activity.

The role of consolidations and acquisitions varied considerably among industries. As is shown in Table 33, the share of merger capitalizations for consolidations varied from one-fifth in ordnance (19) to seven-eighths in textiles (22). In terms of firm disappearances the share of consolidations varied from one-sixth in ordnance to more than nine-tenths in furniture (25). Nor was there a very high correspondence by industry between the two measures of merger activity, capitalizations and disappearances. In fourteen of

TABLE 33

Distribution of Consolidations and Acquisitions by Industry, 1895–1920

Industry	Merger Capitalizations			Firm Disappearance		
	Total (millions of dollars)	Percentage by—			Percentage by—	
		Consolidation	Acquisition	Total	Consolidation	Acquisition
Primary metals (33)	3,855.5	74.9	25.1	634	67.7	32.3
Food and kindred products (20)	1,231.1	80.2	19.8	758	74.8	25.2
Petroleum products (29)	1,038.8	50.6	49.4	170	57.1	42.9
Chemicals (28)	1.032.5	83.2	16.8	360	56.7	43.3
Transportation equipment (37)	960.8	69.6	30.4	270	64.8	35.2
Machinery (except 36) (35)	638.9	72.1	27.9	263	59.3	40.7
Bituminous coal mining (12)	615.5	46.3	53.7	513	83.4	16.6
Metal products (34)	485.4	76.1	23.9	269	75.1	24.9
Metal mining (10)	441.2	71.5	28.5	111	55.9	44.1
Tobacco products (21)	412.9	62.7	37.3	180	31.7	68.3
Textiles (22)	403.3	88.5	11.5	167	69.5	30.5
Petroleum and gas extraction (13)	210.5	75.5	34.5	99	59.6	40.4
Stone, clay, glass products (32)	210.5	77.7	22.3	226	87.6	12.4
Paper and allied products (26)	192.2	82.6	17.4	155	75.5	24.5
Rubber products (30)	162.5	49.8	50.2	36	36.1	63.9
Ice, natural and manufactured	156.9	75.5	24.5	122	79.5	20.5
Electrical machinery, etc. (36)	141.4	72.8	27.2	63	60.3	39.7
Miscellaneous manufacturing (39)	104.3	67.4	32.6	79	70.9	29.1
Nonmetallic minerals mining (14)	95.9	76.7	23.3	119	87.4	12.6
Leather and products (31)	81.1	78.3	21.7	38	65.8	34.2
Nonallocable	73.1	65.7	34.3	57	43.9	56.1
Ordnance (19)	57.8	20.8	79.2	15	16.7	83.3
Lumber (24)	54.4	44.1	55.9	48	70.8	29.2
Instruments (38)	46.0	59.4	40.6	30	56.7	43.3
Printing, publishing (27)	37.9	78.4	21.6	18	77.8	22.2
Furniture, fixtures (25)	26.2	72.5	27.5	36	91.7	8.3
Apparel (23)	12.0	74.7	25.3	5	40.0	60.0
Manufacturing	11,165.6	72.9	27.1	1,270	66.8	33.2
Mining	1,363.2	59.5	40.5	189	77.6	22.4

Source: Appendix B.

61

the twenty-seven two-digit categories the share of consolidations (or acquisitions) in total activity as measured by capitalizations departed by more than 10 percentage points from the share as measured by disappearances. This reflects differences among industries in the composition of merger activity, in the average sizes of merging firms, and in the distribution of the activity between periods of high and low price levels.

The smaller relative role of consolidations in mining merger capitalizations contrasts with the larger role of consolidations in mining merger disappearances. In bituminous coal, consolidations commonly combined many small and medium-sized coal-mining companies while acquisitions more commonly signified the absorption of one big coal company by another. The average size of firms entering bituminous coal consolidations was $550,000, while the average size of bituminous coal acquisitions was $3.9 million. The average disappearance size for all consolidations was $2.05 million, while that for all acquisitions was $2.4 million. On the average, the number of firms entering a bituminous coal consolidation was twelve, while that for all industries was eight.

The shift toward the greater role of acquisitions in total merger activity from 1895 to 1920 was participated in by most industries, as shown in Table 34. The over-all shift was brought about by the majority of industries rather than a few leading industries. Indeed the aggregate percentage for 1915–1920 indicates that, although in two-thirds of the industries acquisitions were preponderant, the over-all totals showed a slight majority for consolidations. It follows that consolidations were still relatively important in the industries leading in merger activity.

In three of the five leading industries a larger share of merger capitalizations during 1915–1920 was accounted for by consolidations than by acquisitions. In one (petroleum products) the role of acquisitions was only slightly greater than that of consolidations. Only in primary metals were acquisitions strongly predominant over consolidations. For the five leading merger industries combined, consolidations clearly played the greater role, accounting for 57 per cent of merger capitalizations.

Size of firm, it might be expected, would be among the determinants of the merger process, with the consolidation form more common in the merger of large firms than small. It is easier to merge small firms by acquisition, as the capital required is less likely to overtax the sources of the acquiring firm. Conversely, new sources of capital may be required in merging large firms, as the capital resources of the firm initiating the merger are less likely to suffice for financing from within the firm. This is especially true of many-firm mergers because the capital required is a function of the number of firms merging.

The data on the size of consolidations and acquisitions permit a rough test of this hypothesis. Table 35 summarizes, for two-digit industries, the average size of firms entering mergers of each type. In all three subperiods the industries in which the average

TABLE 34

Percentage Share of Consolidation Capitalizations in Total Merger Capitalizations, Twenty-Seven Industries, 1895–1920

	Number of Industries			
Percentage Share	1895– 1904	1905– 1914	1915– 1920	1895– 1920
Under 25	1	3	9	1
25 to 50	0	2	9	3
50 to 75	6	10	7	13
75 and over	20	12	2	10
Aggregate percentage	87.2	53.7	52.4	71.5

FIVE LEADING MERGER INDUSTRIES, 1915–1920

Industry	Consolidation Capitalizations as Percentage of Total Merger Capitalizations within the Industry
Petroleum products	47.8
Chemicals	86.1
Primary metals	36.7
Transportation equipment	55.0
Food and kindred products	60.1
Aggregate percentage, 5 industries	57.1
All others	39.8

Source: Appendix B.

TABLE 35

Relative Firm Size: Disappearances by Consolidation and by Acquisition, 1895–1920

	1895– 1904	1905– 1914	1915– 1920
Number of industries with larger average firm size for consolidations than for acquisitions	15	17	12
Industries with data available			
Number	23	24	21
Per cent	65.2	70.8	57.1
Number of firms entering average consolidation	9.0	4.9	3.5

Source: Appendix B

consolidation disappearance (measured in terms of capitalizations) was larger than the average acquisition disappearance were in the majority.

In 1895–1904, consolidations dominated the merger activity of all but one of the two-digit industries, as appeared in Table 33. The union of "wholesale lots" of small firms into consolidations was as common as the union of two or several large firms into consolidations. In this period of very high merger activity, size of firm was therefore probably of less importance in determining the process of merger than in later periods of less intense activity.

SUMMARY

The huge turn-of-the-century merger wave was probably unique in the overwhelming importance of the consolidation form of merger. In neither the 1905–1914 decade of very low activity nor the 1915–1920 period of reviving merger activity did the consolidation resume this dominant role.

The rise in importance of the acquisition form of merger, though not unbroken, claimed some of the characteristics of a secular trend phenomenon. Apart from the very large consolidations which reappeared on the resumption of increased general merger activity in 1915–1920, acquisition merger activity has been a consistently growing share of total merger activity.

Examination of the 1915–1920 revival of merger activity suggests that the consolidation form of merger was more commonly found in industries of sharply increased merger activity. This generalization is encouraged by the predominance of consolidations in almost all industries in the huge turn-of-the-century merger wave.

State of Incorporation

Mergers are governed by state corporation laws, which define the conditions under which a corporation can secure capital, the lines of business in which it can engage, and its power to hold the stock of other corporations. If the corporate charter permits wide latitude in these matters, it will be easy for the firm to engage in merger activity. If the charter is strict, merger will be difficult or impossible.

The liberalization of the corporation laws of a number of states, commencing in the late 1880's, may have helped initiate the high levels of merger activity of the turn of the century and the subsequent establishment of mergers as a continuing phenomenon in the American economy. With the New Jersey Holding Company Act of 1888 a competition arose among several states to induce businesses to incorporate under their laws—largely, no doubt, in order to bolster the states' finances with revenues from incorporation fees.

To observe the pattern of states leading in merger incorporations, and the shifts among the states over time, may suggest the degree to which consolidations activity responded to changes in the corporation laws of different states. The distributions presented below are limited, perforce, to consolidations, which, being new incorporations, were usually reported in the news, with state of incorporation given. The coverage was very low for mergers by acquisition, which rarely formed a new corporation. It should be recalled that the consolidation form of merger declined in relative importance from 1895 to 1920. Accordingly the findings apply to a smaller share of total merger activity in 1915–1920 than in 1895–1904.

The distribution of consolidation activity by state of incorporation is presented in Table 36. Three states, New Jersey, New York, and Delaware, led in consolidation activity over the twenty-six-year period. Together they accounted for 78 per cent of authorized equity capitalizations, 61 per cent of gross firm disappearances by consolidation, and 55 per cent of the consolidations. Of the three, New Jersey was overwhelmingly the leader, accounting for more than two-thirds of the consolidation capitalizations of the three states, more than three-fourths of gross firm disappearances, and more than one-half of the number of consolidations.

The proportion of capitalizations accounted for by New Jersey was almost twice its proportion of the number of consolidations, indicating that a large share of the most highly capitalized consolidations were organized in New Jersey. The excess of the proportion of gross firm disappearances by consolidation over that of the number of consolidations indicates that New Jersey also had more than its proportionate share of many-firm consolidations.

For New York and Delaware consolidations the proportion of capitalizations matched closely the proportion of consolidations, suggesting that these two states did not have more than their share of highly capitalized consolidations. Their lower share of gross firm disappearances relative to their number of consolidations indicates that they had few many-firm mergers.

Much of the contrast between New Jersey on the one hand, and New York and Delaware on the other, is explained by shifts among the leading consolidation states within the twenty-six-year period.

TABLE 36
Distribution of Consolidations by State of Incorporation, 1895–1920
(*per cent*)

State	Consolidation Capitalizations	Gross Firm Disappearances	Number of Consolidations
New Jersey	54.1	47.3	29.6
New York	12.7	7.5	13.5
Delaware	11.2	6.6	11.9
Virginia	2.8	2.8	2.7
Pennsylvania	2.3	7.6	5.2
Maine	1.6	1.9	3.0
West Virginia	1.3	3.5	3.7
Ohio	1.2	2.3	4.0
Illinois	0.9	2.6	1.5
Connecticut	0.9	1.3	1.2
Wyoming	0.9	0.6	0.7
Massachusetts	0.6	1.0	2.8
Missouri	0.5	0.8	1.2
California	0.5	0.7	1.0
Maryland	0.4	0.8	1.0
Michigan	0.4	0.6	0.8
2 states with 3 consolidations each[a]	0.3	0.4	1.0
3 states with 2 consolidations each[b]	0.3	0.7	1.0
14 states with 1 consolidation each[c]	0.9	1.8	2.4
England and Canada	0.1	0.4	0.7
Place of incorporation not given	5.8	8.8	11.4
TOTAL ABSOLUTE CONSOLIDATION ACTIVITY	$9.1 billion	4,444	559

Detail may not add to totals because of rounding.
[a] Rhode Island and Utah.
[b] Indiana, Louisiana, and South Carolina.
[c] Arizona, Colorado, Florida, Georgia, Kansas, Kentucky, Minnesota, North Carolina, Oklahoma, Oregon, South Dakota, Tennessee, Texas, and Washington. The thirteen states for which no consolidations were indicated were Alabama, Arkansas, Idaho, Iowa, Mississippi, Montana, Nebraska, Nevada, New Hampshire, New Mexico, North Dakota, Vermont, and Wisconsin.

As Table 37 reveals, New Jersey dominated the first decade of consolidation activity but became completely inactive in the last six years of the period. New York and Delaware, on the other hand, rose from a minor fraction of 1895–1904 merger activity to share equally in a position of leadership in 1915–1920. Whereas New Jersey accounted for 79.1 per cent of 1895–1904 consolidation capitalizations, New York and Delaware together accounted for 75.3 per cent of 1915–1920 capitalizations. Delaware's rise apparently lagged behind that of New York, as comparison of the 1905–1914 shares of consolidation activity indicates. Examination of the 1915–1920 shares of the two states also suggests that New York had a greater proportion of highly capitalized consolidations than

TABLE 37

Consolidation Activity in Leading States, 1895–1920

Period and Measure of Consolidation Activity	Percentage of Total Consolidation Activity						Total Consolidation Activity
	New Jersey	New York	Delaware	Penn-sylvania	West Virginia	Virginia	Maine	
Capitalizations:								
1895–1904	79.1	3.7	2.6	3.2	0.7	0.6	0.8	$6,026,580,000
1905–1914	20.5	16.3	8.3	1.3	4.8	5.7	8.4	1,184,493,000
1915–1920	0.0	37.1	38.2	0.4	1.0	7.3	0.0	1,905,287,000
Disappearances:								
1895–1904	61.3	5.5	1.9	9.2	1.7	1.9	1.4	3,141
1905–1914	14.4	15.6	6.8	4.4	9.9	3.2	5.5	780
1915–1920	0.0	18.5	34.8	2.8	5.1	8.3	0.0	515
Consolidations:								
1895–1904	50.0	9.7	3.8	7.2	3.1	0.9	2.8	313
1905–1914	12.2	17.3	7.2	3.6	6.5	2.9	6.5	132
1915–1920	0.0	18.6	35.0	2.1	2.1	6.4	0.0	114

Source: Worksheets.

Delaware.[13] This period saw the rise of Delaware among the leading states of incorporation, but not yet to the full ascendancy it later attained.

The foregoing shifts explain the pattern of shares of merger activity shown in Table 36. New Jersey was the leader during the huge turn-of-the-century consolidation wave in which the highly capitalized many-firm consolidation was common. There were twenty consolidations incorporated at $50 million and over in New Jersey in this period, including the $200 million Federal Steel and the $1,370 million U.S. Steel consolidations. Accordingly, New Jersey's share of capitalizations and disappearances exceeded its share of the number of consolidations.

New York and Delaware shared the leadership of the later period, 1915–1920, in which the consolidation of two, three, or four firms was most common. The small number of firm disappearances was compensated by the occurrence of large consolidations in these states. Delaware granted charters to the $50 million Consolidated Textile and $198 million Transcontinental Oil consolidations of 1919, and the $100 million Wheeling Steel consolidation

---

[13] A study of companies listed on the New York Stock and Curb Exchanges in 1932 placed the full ascendancy of the Delaware corporation in the late 1920's. The years 1910–1919 saw Delaware overtake and pass New York and the further decline of New Jersey from its peak in the late 1890's. The period of the leadership of the New York corporation is 1905–1914. See R. C. Larcom, *The Delaware Corporation*, Johns Hopkins Press, 1937, Charts VI and VII, pp. 175–176.

of 1920. New York was the state chosen for incorporation of the $56 million United Motors consolidation of 1916, the $283 million Union Carbide and Carbon consolidation of 1917, and the $283 million Allied Chemical and Dye consolidation of 1920. Virginia accounted for the one remaining very large consolidation of this period with the 1919 incorporation of Invincible Oil at $50 million.

Of the five large consolidations in the middle decade 1905–1914, New Jersey chartered Corn Products Refining ($80 million) in 1906 and General Motors ($60 million) in 1908. The Emerson Brantingham (1912), Goldfield Consolidated Mines (1906), and Tobacco Products (1912) consolidations, each capitalized at $50 million, took place respectively in Illinois, Wyoming, and Virginia.

The variety of industries represented in a state's merger incorporations offers another indication of the attractiveness of its corporation laws. This can be examined, briefly, for several of the leading consolidation states.

New Jersey and Delaware entertained the greatest industrial variety of incorporations, and New York a large variety too. By comparing the numbers of industries incorporated in the three leading states to the number of industries in which more than two consolidations took place (Table 38) we can remove some of the distortion introduced by the several industries of low consolidation activity. Thus compared, the popularity of New Jersey, Delaware, and New York emerges even more clearly.

TABLE 38

Industrial Diversity of Consolidations in Leading States, 1895–1920

(*number of consolidations and of industries*)

	New Jersey	Dela- ware	New York	Penn- sylvania	West Virginia	Industries having—	
						Consoli- dations	More than 2 consoli- dations
1895–1904							
Consolidations	160	12	31	23	10		
Industries	23	9	14	9	8	26	20
1905–1914							
Consolidations	17	10	24	5	9		
Industries	11	9	9	3	3	25	13
1915–1920							
Consolidations	0	49	26	3	3		
Industries	0	16	10	3	3	21	11
1895–1920							
Consolidations	177	71	81	31	22		
Industries	23	21	18	10	8	27	25

Source: Worksheets.

The variety of industries represented by firms consolidating in New Jersey and Delaware was not the result of a wide variety of indigenous industries: both states were small in area and narrow in industrial representation. New York had a relatively wide variety of industries operating within its borders, and part of its popularity can be traced to this fact. By and large, however, the leading states attracted consolidations in industries in which the major share of activity was carried on in other states (Table 39).

Comparisons of the consolidation activity in primary metals and bituminous coal between the three leading incorporation states and two others are presented in Table 40. Pennsylvania and West Virginia were chosen because they were the centers of these two industries of high consolidation activity.

TABLE 39

Consolidations in Leading Incorporation States and in States Leading in Industrial Activity for Selected Industries, 1895–1920

| Industry (SIC) | Number of Consolidations Incorporated in— | | | |
	Leading industrial state[a]	New Jersey	Delaware	New York
Textiles (22)	4 (Mass.)	8	3	5
Iron and steel (331–332)	4 (Pa.)	21	7	3
Motor vehicles (371)	1 (Ohio)	5	6	5
Meat products (201)	1 (Ill.)	0	2	0
Agricultural machinery (352)	1 (Ill.)	3	0	0
Fertilizers (287)	0 (Ga.)	0	2	3
Electrical machinery etc. (36)	0 (Mass.)	4	1	3
Bituminous coal mining (12)	9 (Pa.)	4	2	2

[a] In terms of number of wage earners employed in industry: *Census of Manufactures, 1905*, Bureau of the Census, Vols. III and IV.

TABLE 40

Average Capitalizations and Number of Consolidations in Primary Metals and Bituminous Coal, Five States, 1895–1920

| | State of Incorporation | | | | |
	New Jersey	Delaware	New York	Pennsylvania	West Virginia
AVERAGE CONSOLIDATION CAPITALIZATION (millions of dollars)					
Primary metals	71.5	23.5	6.6	2.4	6.0
Bituminous coal	18.3	7.5	7.7	6.2	6.0
NUMBER OF CONSOLIDATIONS					
Primary metals	31	10	8	5	0
Bituminous coal	4	2	3	9	10

Source: Worksheets.

The leading consolidation states attracted the more highly capitalized consolidations in both industries. The average primary metal consolidation in New Jersey, Delaware, and New York was capitalized at $51.2 million, while in Pennsylvania and West Virginia it was capitalized at $2.4 million. The average bituminous coal capitalization in New Jersey, New York, and Delaware was $12.3 million, while in Pennsylvania and West Virginia it was $6.1 million. Moreover, the leading consolidation states attracted most of the primary metals consolidations, which on the average were more highly capitalized than those in the bituminous coal industry. Most of the smaller bituminous coal consolidations took place in their home states of Pennsylvania and West Virginia.

SUMMARY

The incorporation of consolidations was concentrated in New Jersey, New York, and Delaware. New Jersey dominated the first decade (1895–1904) of the period, but declined to zero activity by 1915. New York and Delaware rose to joint leadership of 1915–1920 consolidation activity, with Delaware lagging behind New York in the middle decade 1905–1914. This shift among the leading states seemed to follow, in a rough way, the shift in the leading states for incorporation activity in general.

The leading incorporation states attracted a wider industrial variety of consolidations than other states. This suggests that corporation laws permitting free choice of lines of business did attract many consolidations that might otherwise have incorporated in their home states.

The most highly capitalized consolidations commonly chose leading incorporation states. This suggests that corporation laws setting higher limits on authorized capitalizations and permitting greater freedom in organizing financial structures attracted the large consolidations.

Chapter 4. The First Merger Wave

A phenomenon as large and widespread as the wave of mergers centering about the peak years of 1899–1901 has called forth many explanations, none of which commanded general acceptance. The data on mergers (and on other important and related economic series) were inadequate for careful tests. Having no even remotely similar precedent, the wave seemed to be historically unique. Thus the phenomenon was explained largely in terms of broad historical developments.

The present examination takes the form of separate empirical tests of relationships between the merger wave and certain historical developments in the United States that have been credited with causing it. Briefly, they are: retardation of industrial growth; the immediately preceding expansion of the national railroad system; the growth of a highly organized capital market; the increase of motivation toward market control. For these developments the data permitted a fairly detailed scrutiny of possible causal relationships. Other major theories could not be considered because of the lack of relevant data.

Relationship to Industrial Retardation

A popular explanation of the early merger movement is that it marked a period in United States economic development in which retardation of growth set in. Mergers, in this context, were interpreted as devices whereby producers could preserve profits in the face of slackening demand and greater pressures of competition. One of the principal exponents of this thesis, Myron Watkins, described the process as follows:

> The opening of a new and wider market involves pioneering costs which call for the compact association of producers. But once a new market has been opened by the joint action of the associated producers, its development attracts the ambition and varied talents of many producers, the prizes for successful competition being high. The third and final phase is reached when the limit of the expansion of a given market has been touched, and the amount and character of its consumption have become settled and known. The gains from initiative and ingenuity are then no longer sufficient to hold producers upon an independent course, and they fall in together for their common enrichment at the expense of consumers.[1]

[1] Myron Watkins, *Industrial Combinations and Public Policy*, Cambridge, 1927, pp. 12–13.

Watkins went on to describe the historical trends to which he attributed the retardation in market growth: the closing of the frontier, the slackening of population growth, the slowing of technological change, and the post-1873 secular decline in prices. In his view, these various tendencies converged at the end of the nineteenth century and set the stage for the merger movement, which he described as "a centralizing phase in the organization of industrial control in the United States."[2]

A thorough test of this hypothesis would involve examination of the cycles of industry growth in the United States, a project much too ambitious to undertake here. Instead, a more limited analysis is offered, which derives its value from examination of specific data on the general patterns of industrial growth in the period before 1895, the growth patterns in industries having high merger activity, and the relation of these patterns to the first merger wave.

Proponents of the retardation thesis have properly emphasized that it is retardation in individual industries rather than retardation in aggregate industrial growth that is important in merger behavior. However, they failed to deal seriously with the next logical step in the thesis, determination of the degree of retardation necessary to compel firms to merge. This omission is understandable, because the tools for predicting competitive behavior are certainly not sharp enough for the task. What the retardation thesis seems to imply, in this respect, is that at the turn of the century there was a change in the pattern of industrial growth of sufficient magnitude or abruptness to force competitors to band together to alleviate the ruinous tendencies of falling demand and drastic price decline. The retardation would have had to take the form of either an absolute decline in production or a drastic drop in the rate of growth prevailing in the period just preceding the merger wave. If the decline were more gradual, it would be difficult to demonstrate that, at a certain date, the retardation had reached that critical level at which firms were compelled to merge. We shall look to see if (1) there was a marked increase in general retardation just preceding the merger movement, and if (2) the industries characterized by high merger activity were in fact those experiencing retardation.

Before testing the growth retardation–merger thesis, let us briefly examine the way in which retardation has been measured. The data are taken from Arthur F. Burns's study of production

2 *Ibid.*, p. 16.

trends in the United States.[3] They relate to the rate of growth of various series of production data for overlapping decades (eleven years) from 1870 through 1930. The first decade for which growth is measured is 1870–1880, in which 1875 is the central year; the second decade is 1875–1885, and so on. Exponential trends were fitted to the annual data for each of the decades, and the rate of growth was taken from the trend equations thus obtained.

In terms of these rates of growth data, retardation exists if successive decades are consistently characterized by rates of growth lower than the rates of the decades preceding them. Burns found retardation, thus defined, to have been the overwhelmingly common pattern of industry growth in the period 1870–1930.[4]

THE GENERAL PATTERN OF GROWTH

If retardation was a factor in the turn-of-the-century merger movement, there should appear at least sustained retardation in the period immediately preceding the merger wave. Sharply increased retardation would of course be a stronger indication that retardation was a factor. The evidence available to measure the change in industry growth is found in Burns's study, from which Table 41 is reproduced. It includes production series of industries in agriculture and fisheries, mining, manufactures and construction, transportation and trade, thus providing a general picture of the pattern of growth.

The table shows that the two overlapping decades immediately preceding the period of merger activity at the turn of the century, 1890–1900 and 1895–1905, saw the stabilization or reversal of the pattern of retardation characteristic of the decades preceding them. This appears in the proportion of series experiencing an increase at the rate of 10 per cent or more per year, and also in the proportion of series experiencing a negative rate of increase. The decade 1890–1900 saw stabilization in the proportion of series experiencing a rate of increase of 10 per cent or more. The decade 1895–1905 saw a substantial increase in the proportion of the high growth rate series. Comparison of the proportions of increases of 10 per cent and over for the three decades 1900–1910, 1905–1915,

---

[3] Arthur F. Burns, *Production Trends in the United States Since 1870*, National Bureau of Economic Research, 1934, Chapter III.

[4] Burns also demonstrated the existence of long-run cycles in the secular trend, which he called trend-cycles. He showed their existence by comparing the decade exponential trend rates with the decade rates of what he called the primary trend (*Ibid.*, pp. 175ff.). Adjustment to take account of the long-cycle factor is not required, however, for present purposes; the change in growth patterns that business firms respond to is the gross effect of retardation and trend cycles.

TABLE 41

Increases and Decreases in Production Growth Rates, by Overlapping Decades,
1870–1930

Decade	Total Number of Series Covered	Rates of 10 per cent and Over		Rates of 0 or Less	
		Number of series	Percentage of series covered	Number of series	Percentage of series covered
1870–1880	66	16	24.2	6	9.1
1875–1885	69	20	29.0	5	7.2
1880–1890	97	17	17.5	8	8.2
1885–1895	104	11	10.6	10	9.6
1890–1900	104	10	9.6	8	7.7
1895–1905	104	21	20.2	8	7.7
1900–1910	104	8	7.7	11	10.6
1905–1915	104	4	3.8	17	16.3
1910–1920	104	9	8.7	22	21.3
1915–1925	102	5	4.9	43	42.2
1920–1930	102	6	5.9	26	25.5

Source: Arthur F. Burns, *Production Trends in the United States Since 1870*, National Bureau of Economic Research, 1934, p. 81, Table 13.

and 1910–1920 indicates that the high rate of increase carried well into the twentieth century, probably, at least until the end of high merger activity in 1905.[5]

These data do not reveal the pattern of growth to be expected if the retardation thesis were valid, for the pattern found was marked by neither a continuation of the retardation nor by its marked increase. Indeed, the data reveal quite the opposite picture.

The pattern of changes in Table 41 shows a marked decline in the rate of growth in the 1905–1915 decade. This roughly coincides with the decade of low merger activity from 1905 through 1914. Further, the resumption of higher growth rates in the period 1915–1920 was accompanied by a revival of merger activity. Thus it appears that merger activity was more commonly found in periods of increased general acceleration than in periods of increased retardation in industry growth.

It is dangerous, however, to infer from these findings that industrial growth retardation had no positive connection with

[5] The one and one-half decades preceding the high merger activity of the late 1920's also saw a reversal of the retardation pattern (Table 41). Moreover, the general acceleration of the late 1920's might be understated by Burns's sample, which does not include more recently founded industries and thus may indicate a fictitiously low number of rapidly growing series. A good case probably could be made against the growth-retardation–merger thesis by a detailed examination of the growth rates of high-merger industries in this later period.

mergers. Mergers were prominent in only some of these industries. It is important to know whether the industries of high merger activity were among those characterized by increasing or decreasing rates of growth preceding the initiation of mergers. We turn now to this question.

GROWTH RATES IN INDUSTRIES OF HIGH MERGER ACTIVITY

The data provided by Burns's study permit the testing of the growth-retardation–merger hypothesis for the specific industries in which the greater amount of merger activity took place. Of the seventy-seven series in mining and manufacturing which Burns presents, forty-four are related directly to industries in which there was a high degree of merger activity. Only three two-digit industries of high merger activity—paper and allied products, fabricated metal products, and machinery (except electrical)—had no relevant production series. The industries having high merger activity in 1895–1904 and the number of production series relating to them are presented in Table 42. In terms of firm disappearances, the

TABLE 42

Production Series Related to Industries with High Merger Activity, 1895–1904

Industry	Net Firm Disappearances	Number of Relevant Production Series
Food and kindred products (20)	524	8
Tobacco products (21)	133	4
Chemicals (28)	221	3
Stone, glass (32) and nonmetallic minerals (14)	276	5
Iron and steel mills, foundries and mines (331, 332, 101)	391	6
Nonferrous smelting, refining, foundries, mines (333–336, 102–104)	85	13
Transportation equipment (37)	127	2
Bituminous coal mining (12)	305	3
Metal products (34)	185	0
Machinery, except electrical (35)	142	0
Paper and allied products (26)	116	0

Source: Worksheets and Table C-2.

eight industries for which relevant production series are available accounted for 83 per cent of all 1895–1904 merger activity, and for 92 per cent of the merger activity in those industries having more than forty disappearances. They were also the industries of highest merger activity relative to industry size.

75

The trend of the growth rate pattern for the forty-four production series applicable to the eight industries of greatest merger activity is presented in Table 43. It gives the same kind of information that was presented in Table 41 for the 104 series included there, but Table 43 is more detailed in that it also shows the trend in the 0 to 5 per cent and 5 to 10 per cent classes of growth rates, as well as in the other two classes of 10 per cent and over and below 0 per cent.

Table 43 reveals that the period immediately preceding the intense merger activity beginning in 1898 was characterized by

TABLE 43

Annual Growth Rates of Industries with High 1895–1904
Relative Merger Activity, by Overlapping Decades, 1870–1915

Decade	Total Number of Series Covered	Percentage of Series by Average Annual Growth Rate of Output			
		10% or more	5.0–9.9 %	0.0–4.9 %	Less than 0
1870–1880	23	26.1	43.5	21.7	8.7
1875–1885	24	37.5	45.9	8.3	8.3
1880–1890	38	18.4	44.7	34.2	2.7
1885–1895	44	9.1	43.1	45.5	2.3
1890–1900	44	11.4	43.1	41.0	4.5
1895–1905	44	31.8	47.7	18.2	2.3
1900–1910	44	11.3	41.0	41.0	6.7
1905–1915	44	6.8	25.0	59.1	9.1

Source: Table C-2.

acceleration rather than retardation in the growth of the industries of high merger activity. In the three overlapping decades 1885–1895, 1890–1900, and 1895–1905 there were successively larger decade-rates of growth. The proportion of series experiencing annual rates of growth of more than 10 per cent increased from 9.1 per cent to 31.9 per cent of the total number of series. The proportion of series experiencing a 5.0 to 9.9 per cent rate of growth increased from 43.2 per cent to 47.8 per cent of the total. The proportion of the total number of series experiencing a less than 5 per cent rate of growth decreased from 47.8 per cent to 20.5 per cent of the total.

After the 1895–1905 decade the retardation resumes, but not sufficiently to offset the preceding acceleration. The decade 1900–1910 saw a return to the growth-rate pattern of the 1885–1895 decade, and not to the lower growth rates that a projection of the pre-1885 retardation pattern would signify. Thus a substantial increase in retardation does not reappear until after the period of high merger activity. The growth rates for individual high merger industries bear out these findings. As Table 44 shows, in none of the eight industries

TABLE 44

Average Annual Percentage Rates of Growth for Eight Industries of High 1895–1907
Merger Activity, by Overlapping Decades, 1870–1915

						Decade			
Industry	No. of Series	1870–1880	1875–1885	1880–1890	1885–1895	1890–1900	1895–1905	1900–1910	1905–1915
Food (20)	8	4.66	6.58	4.58	5.30	3.70	6.53	2.58	2.73
Tobacco (21)	4	3.30	5.50	8.13	4.75	2.13	3.30	4.80	5.05
Chemicals (28)	3	13.75	15.85	6.70	5.73	7.57	6.33	5.07	3.27
Stone, glass, etc. (32, 14)	5	...	...	11.68	8.72	13.62	20.72	11.20	6.16
Iron and steel (331–332, 101)	6	12.28	10.20	7.92	3.43	4.35	9.85	5.18	3.92
Transportation equipment (37)	2	−4.1	−3.7	1.1	0.55	1.3	13.15	−0.55	4.35
Nonferrous metals (333–336, 102–104)	13	9.06	7.90	5.95	10.15	9.02	7.88	4.74	5.34
Bituminous coal (121)	3	5.25	11.45	8.00	5.10	5.87	9.07	6.07	3.70

Source: Table C-2.

was there an appreciable increase in retardation in the three decades 1885–1895, 1890–1900, and 1895–1905. Four of the eight industries (32 and 14; 331–332 and 101; 37; and 121) enjoyed a sustained acceleration over this period. Two (20, 21) saw a reversal of a previous pattern of retardation. In one (28), the 1895–1905 rate of growth was higher than the 1885–1895 rate but lower than the 1890–1900 rate. Only one industry, nonferrous metals (manufacturing, 333–336, and mining, 102–104), experienced a sustained retardation over the three overlapping decades. It is noteworthy that merger activity in nonferrous metals remained at a fairly high level in the decade 1905–1914, while that of most other industries dropped off sharply after 1902. Thus the 1905–1915 acceleration of nonferrous production coincided with a relative increase of nonferrous merger activity.

CONCLUSION

Statistical examination of the growth-retardation–merger relationship indicates that there is little empirical basis for believing that the turn-of-the-century merger wave was caused by a general retardation in industry growth thought to be prevalent at that time. The last one and one-half decades of the nineteenth century saw the halting and reversing of the previous decline in growth rates for industry in general. In the industries of high merger activity, the reversal of retardation was even more pronounced than it was for industry in general. Measured on an industry-by-industry basis, retardation was generally absent from industries of highest merger activity in the decade and one-half preceding the merger wave. Indeed, these findings suggest that more satisfactory explanations of merger movements may be found in periods of accelerating growth than in periods of retardation. This possibility is explored in more detail in Chapter 5.

England had a large merger wave almost simultaneous with the early American movement. Apparently the merger wave in Britain, like that in the United States, occurred during a period of acceleration rather than of retardation. The British experience is presented in detail in Appendix A.

Development of the Transportation System

Another frequent explanation for the merger movement at the end of the nineteenth century is the achievement of a national network of railroads at that time. This brought about a fundamental change in the nature of markets for goods, it is held. Producers now found it possible to sell their goods in wider markets, thus bringing themselves into more direct competition with other producers who previously had enjoyed a degree of geographical isolation. One of the principal exponents of the thesis, Joe S. Bain, summarized the development as follows:

"Competition was intensified by the continuing growth of the railroad systems, which tended to bring all of the principal firms together in direct competition for a single national market. The economy was passing from a situation where a fairly large number of small manufacturers sold their products, each in a limited local market somewhat protected by high costs of transportation, to a situation where a few large firms vied among themselves for sales in a single market. In the new environment, price competition was potentially ruinous to all."[6]

[6] Joe S. Bain, "Industrial Concentration and Government Anti-Trust Policy," in *The Growth of the American Economy*, H. F. Williamson, ed., Prentice-Hall, 1944, p. 710.

In this view, producers combined to eliminate increasing competition. Through merger, ruinous price competition could be avoided, and the markets for their products could be "stabilized."

Running through much of the transportation growth–merger hypothesis, and frequently taken as an inseparable part of it, is the argument that the development of national markets permitted the realization of economies of scale in production. This argument will not be examined here for the following reasons. First, the empirical examination of scale economies is much too complex to permit a satisfactory analysis in this limited study.[7] Second, transportation improvement is only one of the ways by which the market expansion needed to realize economies of scale can be achieved. Population growth within fixed geographical regions, cultural change, and per capita income growth are factors of possibly greater importance. Brief comment on the significance of scale economies is made in a later section. The present task is to examine transportation development as a cause of mergers, apart from economies of scale.

PLAN OF EMPIRICAL EXAMINATION

If transportation growth favored mergers we should expect the industries in which the greatest merger activity occurred to have the following characteristics: First, the product would be of such nature that per-mile transportation costs are fairly large relative to product price. Reduced transportation costs would produce a large relative change in delivered prices in distant markets, and thus provide the stimulus required to induce faraway producers to meet the prices of near-by producers. Second, the production of the product would be quite widely dispersed. If all producers were located in the same small geographical area a decline in transportation costs would not change the character of the competition; it would already be a national market in the sense that all sellers could compete for the patronage of all buyers.

To test the validity of the transportation growth–merger hypothesis in this context, three separate factors in the relationship will be examined. First, it must be determined whether, as a matter of fact, the transportation network did expand, and transportation costs did decline, in the years preceding the merger movement. If these developments did not occur, or if there were only a small growth in transportation, the hypothesis would fail for lack of a causal factor.

---

[7] Some observations concerning their significance are given in a later section of the chapter.

Second, given the underlying pre-merger transportation developments, it is then necessary to determine the proportion of the merger movement accounted for by industries having high per-mile transportation costs relative to the price of the product. This provides a rough measure of the proportion of total merger activity that could have occurred in response to declines in transportation cost. If this share is relatively small, the transportation growth factor can have played only a contributory rather than a dominant role in the movement.

Third, it must be determined whether the industries with high per-mile transportation costs relative to product price had widely dispersed producing centers. If these industries were concentrated in relatively small geographical areas, then reductions in transportation costs would not alter the effective market areas of firms relative to each other.

PRE-MERGER TRENDS IN TRANSPORTATION GROWTH

The data describing transportation growth apply to railroads only. This was the overwhelmingly important form of inter-regional freight transportation in the last two decades of the nineteenth century. It was also the only form of transportation for which comprehensive detailed data were available.

The development of the railroad transportation system and the trend in freight rates and wholesale prices are described in Table 45. The period 1882–1900 saw a large absolute expansion in the railroad system. Miles of track increased from 114,400 to 193,000, or by 69 per cent. Ton-miles of freight carried increased from 39.3 million to 141.6 million, an increase of 260 per cent. The cost of freight transportation dropped from 1.236 cents per ton-mile in 1882 to 0.729 cents in 1900, a drop of 41 per cent.

It is not possible to compare the 1882–1900 changes with transportation growth of earlier periods since data on freight ton-miles and revenue per ton-mile are unavailable before 1882. However, the 1882–1900 development can be compared with that of the post-1900 period. The period 1900–1916, being comparable in length to the 1882–1900 period and preceding the World War I period of rapidly increased activity, was chosen. The comparisons are presented in Table 45. The data are of average annual rates of change computed, using the compound-interest formula, from the values for the initial and terminal years of each period.

The data presented in the table indicate a higher rate of railroad transportation growth in 1882–1900 than in 1900–1916. This was true for both miles of track and for ton-miles of freight hauled.

80

TABLE 45

Railroad Mileage, Freight Ton-Miles, Freight Revenue per Ton-Mile, and Wholesale Prices, 1882–1916

Year	Railroad Mileage (thousands of miles)	Freight Ton-Miles (millions)		Freight Revenue per Ton-Mile (cents)		Wholesale Price Index (BLS, 1926 = 100)
1882	114.4	39.3		1.236		66.1
1884	125.1	44.7		1.124		60.5
1886	133.6	52.8		1.042		56.0
1888	154.2	65.4		0.977		57.4
1890[a]	163.4	79.2	76.2	0.927	0.941	56.2
1892		171.6	88.2		0.898	52.2
1894		178.7	80.3		0.860	47.9
1896		182.8	95.3		0.806	46.5
1898		186.4	114.1		0.753	48.5
1900		193.3	141.6		0.729	56.1
1902		202.5	157.3		0.757	58.9
1904		213.9	174.5		0.780	59.7
1906		224.4	215.9		0.748	61.8
1908		233.5	218.4		0.754	62.9
1910		240.3	255.0		0.753	70.4
1912		246.8	264.1		0.744	69.1
1914		252.1	288.8		0.737	68.1
1916		254.3	383.5		0.719	85.5

AVERAGE ANNUAL PERCENTAGE RATES OF CHANGE:

Period	Railroad Mileage	Freight Ton-Miles	Intensity of Track Utilization	Revenue per Ton-Mile	Wholesale Prices
1882–1900	+3.0	+7.3	+4.3	−3.7	−0.9
1900–1916	+1.9	+5.8	−3.9	no appreciable change	+2.7

[a] The two values for 1890 represent a shift in data sources. For the period 1882–1890 the Interstate Commerce Commission compiled railroad statistics from annual issues of *Poor's Manual of Railroads*. From 1890 forward the data were compiled from the direct reports of railroads to the I.C.C.

Source for railroad statistics: *Historical Statistics of the United States, 1789–1945*, Bureau of the Census, 1949, pp. 200, 203, Series K-2, 15, 16, 29, 45, and 47.

However, some of the growth in track mileage may have duplicated existing railroad connections. This is suggested by the fact that the rate of growth in the intensity of track utilization was only slightly larger in 1882–1900 than in 1900–1916. The development for the whole period before and after the merger wave primarily represented the progressive rail saturation of limited geographical areas rather than the tying together of distant markets.[8]

[8] However, most pre-1882 economic activity was centered in the northeastern section of the country. The filling-in of the rail network may thus have had a greater effect on competition than the extension of the transcontinental rail lines through the sparsely populated and economically small western part of the country.

The cost of rail freight transportation, as indicated by revenue per ton-mile, dropped at an average rate of 3.7 per cent per year in the eighteen years preceding the turn of the century, and remained essentially constant in the sixteen years following 1900. In absolute terms the pre-1900 and post-1900 changes were distinct. However, relative to the wholesale price level of commodities, the price of rail freight transportation declined at about the same rate in 1882–1900 and 1900–1916. From 1882 to 1900 revenue per ton-mile declined markedly, while wholesale prices declined moderately. From 1900 to 1916 revenue per ton-mile remained constant, while wholesale prices rose substantially. In both periods the annual percentage change in revenue per ton-mile was about 2.8 points below that of wholesale prices.

These findings thus suggest that transportation growth in the decade and one-half before the merger wave was not radically different from that in the decade and one-half following it. In both periods the growth was large and represented intensive rather than extensive growth in the railroad system. There was a sustained fall in the relative price of transportation all through the period, with no sharp break in 1900. The somewhat larger pre-1900 rate of growth might have made it more likely that a merger wave would occur about 1900 rather than later. However, the evolutionary pattern of development throughout the period indicates that this difference was probably unimportant.

It is probable that the pre-1882 growth of railroads was even more rapid than the 1882–1900 growth. Thus, while it can be argued on this theory that the merger wave would have been less likely to occur after 1900, there is no equally strong evidence that it could not have occurred considerably earlier than 1900. Probably any period from 1875 to 1900 could be characterized as following upon a decade of very rapid transportation growth.

MERGER ACTIVITY AND TRANSPORTATION COSTS

While transportation growth in 1882–1900 was not greatly different from that of the period following, it was, nevertheless, large and significant. Therefore further exploration of the transportation growth–merger relationship is of interest, and we turn to the question whether mergers occurred in industries we would expect to respond more vigorously to changes in transportation costs— i.e., in industries where transportation costs are high, but not prohibitive, relative to the price of the product.

In order to demonstrate the incidence of high and low transportation costs among industries in which merger activity occurred, the following breakdown by transportation costs has been made:

1. Industries with a characteristically local market
2. Industries with low transportation costs relative to price of product
3. Industries with high transportation costs relative to price of product
4. Industries for which the role of transportation costs could not be clearly ascertained

The first category, local market industries, includes breweries, firms producing brick, sand and gravel, crushed stone, ice, and the like. The extreme weight and bulk of the products, and the ubiquity of their source materials have restricted their markets to local areas despite marked reductions in transportation costs. This category also includes highly perishable products. The second category, industries with national markets but low transportation costs in relation to price of product, contains nonperishable and semi-perishable products whose production involved complex preparation processes. The third category, industries with national markets and high transportation costs, includes basic minerals and products of large bulk and weight with a low degree of fabrication. It also includes products such as sheet glass which, by virtue of their fragility, involve high transportation costs. The fourth, non-allocable, category includes nonperishable products of low bulk and weight, with a moderate degree of fabrication, and highly fabricated but bulky products. In this category were also placed those products whose transportation cost characteristics were too unclear (to the writer) to allow assignment to another category. The detailed breakdown by industry and product is presented in Table C-3.

The breakdown of merger activity by the role of transportation costs is summarized in Table 46. The measure of merger activity used is firm disappearances by consolidation and acquisition. From the table it can be seen that at least a majority of mergers occurred in industries in which transportation costs were an important factor in the delivered price of the product. One of 2,546 firm disappearances which could be allocated to a major or minor transportation-importance category, 1,457, or 57 per cent, occurred in industries where transportation costs were important. The remaining 1,089 disappearances, or 43 per cent, occurred in industries where a reduction in transportation costs could be expected to have had little effect. In calculations based on the consolidation series only,

TABLE 46

Merger Activity in Terms of Relative Importance of Transportation Costs
to the Industry, 1895–1904

	Firm Disappearances		Percentage of Total Disappearances	
Transportation costs of—	All merger activity	Consolidations only	All merger activity	Consolidations only
Major importance	1,457	1,258	48.4	50.5
Minor importance				
Local Industries	304	289	10.1	11.6
National industries: low				
transportation costs	785	573	26.1	23.0
Importance not ascertained	466	373	15.5	15.0
	3,012	2,493	100.0	100.0

Data for consolidations are listed separately (and examined separately throughout this test of the transportation hypothesis) because of the large differences in cut-off limits imposed on the consolidations and acquisitions series (see Chapter 2). There was the risk that measures of total merger activity might contain appreciable numbers of acquisitions of small firms, not comparable in size to consolidation disappearances, a factor that might weaken the test. Detail may not add to totals because of rounding.
Source: Table C-3.

59 per cent of allocable disappearances occurred in industries in which transportation costs were important.

The proportion of merger activity in which transportation cost reductions may have had an effect is sufficiently large to warrant further investigation. However, a substantial share of merger activity occurred in industries in which transportation cost declines would not have had an appreciable effect. Therefore it cannot be concluded, on the basis of this evidence, that mergers occurred in high transport-cost industries with greater intensity than in low transport-cost industries. The next section brings other evidence to bear.

GEOGRAPHICAL CONCENTRATION AND MERGER ACTIVITY

The transportation growth–merger thesis implies that high transport-cost industries exhibiting merger activity would have widely dispersing producing centers. If most producers were concentrated in small geographical areas there would be no exclusive local markets for reduced transportation costs to destroy.

At the same time, there is some logical reason to expect that high per-mile transportation costs and geographical concentration should go together. Firms with high transportation costs are forced to locate in those usually restricted areas which are optimally located with respect to materials, power and labor resources, and

84

buyers. Thus, on the purely technical grounds of cost minimization, we should expect to find higher geographical concentration in industries with high per-mile transportation costs than in those with lower costs. It follows that we might expect to find closer proximity of firms in those very industries in which transport-cost reductions are supposed to break down barriers between distant firms. Thus the historical decline in transport costs might be credited wrongly with achieving a condition which already existed. This is merely an exercise in deductive logic, however. We shall do better to examine the empirical evidence.

An indication of the greater geographical concentration of high transport-cost industries is provided in Table 47. The geographical

TABLE 47

Geographical Concentration of Manufacturing among Industries Classified by the Size of Transportation Costs Relative to Product Price, 1895–1904

Transportation Costs Relative to Product Price	Number of Industries	Average Index of Geographical Concentration	
		Simple	Weighted[a]
High	10	0.510	0.557
Low	6	.477	.479
Local markets	?	.312	.293
Cost not ascertained	5	.451	.454
Total	23	.471	.511

[a] Weighted by net firm disappearances.

Source: Tables C-3 and C-4.

concentration of an industry was measured by using, as an index, the proportion of industry wage-earner employment in the three adjoining states of highest employment. These indexes were derived from the *1905 Census of Manufactures* for 23 two- and three-digit industries for which merger activity was recorded. The industries accounted for 1,676 net disappearances, or 68.5 per cent of the 2,445 net manufacturing disappearances of 1895–1904. Among these industries the high transport-cost industries showed higher geographical concentration than either low transport-cost industries or merger industries in general.

To determine more directly whether there was a negative relationship between merger activity and geographical concentration, as the transportation growth–merger thesis implies, a correlation analysis was made. It was possible to correlate relative merger activity with geographical concentration for twenty two- and three-digit industries. The comparison is presented in Table 48. It can

TABLE 48
Relative Merger Activity and Geographical Concentration for Twenty Industries, 1895-1904

| | Relative Merger Activity[a] | | |
Standard Industrial Classification	All merger activity	Consolidations only	Geographical Concentration
Meat products (201)	0.294	0.013	0.547
Dairy products (202)	.201	1.38	.290
Canning fruits and vegetables (203)	.786	.728	.307
Grain mill products (204)	.153	.138	.247
Tobacco products (21)	.949	.573	.543
Textiles (22)	.136	.135	.480
Lumber and furniture (24-25)	.083	.068	.180
Paper and allied products (26)	.561	.540	.455
Printing, publishing (27)	.031	.026	.336
Industrial organic chemicals (282)	.061	.041	.280
Paints (285)	.334	.324	.542
Fertilizers (287)	.953	.746	.274
Petroleum (291)	.007	.007	.365
Leather (311)	.163	.159	.505
Glass (321-323)	.402	.398	.636
Iron and steel (331-332)	2.505	2.311	.688
Farm machinery (352)	.730	.709	.518
Electrical machinery etc. (36)	.439	.388	.571
Motor vehicles (371)	2.190	1.654	.507
Ship and Boat building (373)	.342	.328	.348
Coefficient of rank correlation:[b]			
All merger activity	+0.421		
Consolidations only	+0.479		

[a] Measured as ratio of merger capital to industry capital. For a more detailed description of this measure see Chapter 2.

[b] Both coefficients of correlation are significant at the 5 per cent level but not at the 1 per cent level of significance.

Source: Table C-4.

be seen that a moderate degree of positive relationship existed between the merger activity of an industry and its geographical concentration, which suggests that less intensive merger activity occurred in industries in which producing centers were widely dispersed.

When the high- and low-transport cost industries are examined separately, the negative relation between geographical concentration and merger activity suggested by the transportation growth–merger hypothesis is further contradicted, as Table 49 shows. The average relative merger activity in high-transport cost industries (0.620 and 0.528) is lower than that in low-transport cost industries (0.721 and 0.574). Moreover, the rank correlation between mergers and geographical concentration in high-transport cost industries is

TABLE 49

Relative Merger Activity and Geographical Concentration in Fifteen Industries with High and Low Transportation Costs, 1895–1904

	High Transport Cost			Low Transport Cost		
	Relative Merger Activity		Geographical concentration	Relative Merger Activity		Geographical concentration
Standard industrial classification	All merger activity	Consolidations only		All merger activity	Consolidation only	
201	0.294	0.013	0.547	0.949	0.573	0.543
204	.153	.138	.247	.061	.041	.280
24–5	.083	.068	.180	.334	.324	.542
26	.561	.540	.455	.730	.709	.518
287	.953	.746	.274	.439	.388	.571
291	.007	.007	.365	2.190	1.654	.507
321–3	.402	.398	.636	.342	.328	.348
331–2	2.505	2.311	.688			
Standard industrial classification				21		
				282		
				285		
				352		
				36		
				371		
				373		

Average relative merger activity:

	All merger activity	Consolidation only
High transport-cost industries	0.620	0.528
Low transport-cost industries	0.721	0.574

Coefficient of rank correlation between merger activity and geographical concentration:

	All merger activity	Consolidation only
High transport-cost industries	+0.571	+0.327
Low transport-cost industries	+0.357	+0.286

Source: Table C-4.

higher ($+0.571$ and $+0.327$) than in low-transport cost industries ($+0.357$ and $+0.286$). While the sampling reliability of this test is small, the findings are nonetheless opposite to the comparison that the transportation growth–merger hypothesis would lead us to expect.[9] High-transport cost industries should, on that theory, exhibit a more negative merger–geographical concentration correlation than that exhibited by low-transport cost industries.

CONCLUSION

From an empirical examination of the relationship between the growth of the railroad transportation system and the 1895–1904 merger movement certain relationships have been demonstrated. First, the merger wave occurred during a large and protracted expansion of the railroad system, and during a substantial decline in the relative cost of transportation. Second, a considerable part of total 1895–1904 merger activity in manufacturing and mining took place in those industries in which transportation costs were large relative to the price of the product.

However, the geographical concentration of high-transport cost industries was higher than that for low-transport cost industries, suggesting that there were few geographical barriers to be broken down by transportation cost reductions. Moreover. while the transportation growth–merger hypothesis would lead us to expect a negative relationship between merger activity and geographical concentration, the results show a positive relationship between them. The relationship was more positive for industries with high transport costs than for those with low transport costs, again in contradiction to what we would expect if transportation growth had a significant effect on merger behavior. The findings therefore cast doubt on the theory that mergers occurred principally among firms that had seen the growth of transportation destroy their local markets, formerly protected by the barriers of high transport costs.

It appears that the high proportion of merger activity occurring in industries with high transport costs was not due to reductions in these costs. The more correct interpretation seems to be that the industries in which merger activity occurred were only incidentally those with high transport costs. Since mergers occurred in a number of important industries and since these industries

[9] The samples are too small to permit firm conclusions to be drawn from the comparisons. Neither correlation departs significantly from zero at either the 1 per cent or the 5 per cent level of significance. The difference between the two correlation coefficients is likewise not statistically significant.

were as commonly characterized by high as by low transportation costs, it follows that a substantial part of merger activity involved industries with high transportation costs. Beyond this, however, no cause and effect inference seems justified.

Examination of the English merger movement indicates that in England, too, transportation factors were not likely to have been important (see Appendix A). The significant developments in English transportation occurred too many decades before the merger movement to be credited with playing an important role in mergers.

The Capital Market

Another common explanation of the timing of the early merger wave is the development in the United States of an organized large-scale capital market. The existence by the late 1890's of a large capital market has been held necessary for the absorption of the large securities issues of the multimillion dollar consolidations of the era. A corollary thesis is that an organized capital market was the milieu in which financiers and promoters could marshal the financial power needed to induce or coerce independent firms to surrender their independence and enter the large consolidations. Without a highly developed market for capital, it is argued, the large, highly capitalized consolidations of the period would have been difficult, if not impossible to accomplish.

The emergence of the merger movement is so intricately interwoven with concurrent developments in the capital market as to prohibit simple cause and effect explanations. It has been argued with persuasiveness that an organized large-scale capital market was a prerequisite for absorbing the large securities issues of the multimillion dollar consolidations of the era.[10] On the other hand it has been argued that the formation of many new highly capitalized consolidations was the substance upon which the capital market fed in its rapid growth to maturity.[11] Conclusive tests of these relationships are beyond the scope of this study. Instead a brief description of the growth of the securities markets in this period is offered, as a context in which to place subsequent examinations of specific aspects of the capital market–merger relationship.

10 See, for example, George J. Stigler, "Monopoly and Oligopoly by Merger," *Papers and Proceedings of the American Economic Association*, May 1950, pp. 27–31.

11 T. R. Navin and M. V. Sears, "The Rise of a Market For Industrial Securities, 1887–1902," *The Business History Review*, June 1955.

The growth of the capital market in the years leading up to the merger movement is reflected in the growth of the New York Stock Exchange. From the years following the Civil War until the mid-1890's the number of stock issues listed rose almost continuously (Chart 4). An increasing number of firms, mainly railroads, elected

CHART 4

Number of Listed Stock Issues and Number of Stock Shares Traded, New York Stock Exchange, 1874–1918

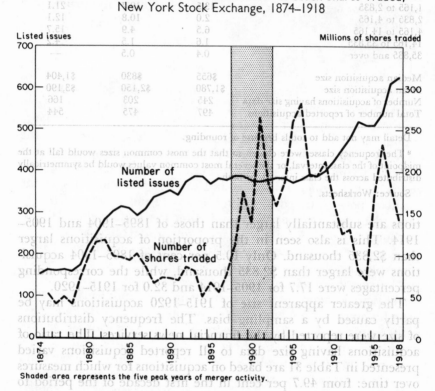

Shaded area represents the five peak years of merger activity.

to seek the wider sources of funds available by listing securities on the organized exchange. In contrast to the growth in the number of issues, the period 1882–1896 exhibited a decline in the total number of shares traded. The average volume of trading per issue therefore declined markedly. Railroad stocks dominated the Exchange in this period as industrials had not yet gained general acceptance among investors.[12] It was therefore principally the rail-

[12] *Ibid.*

90

road issues that suffered from the progressively more shallow market. This period was followed by the extensive railroad reorganizations of the 1890's, largely under the leadership of J. P. Morgan.[13]

After 1895 the number of listed issues leveled off, while trading activity rose sharply; the market for the average issue became much deeper than before. These changes probably reflected two developments. First, the extensive railroad reorganizations succeeded in replacing many small railroad issues with fewer large issues. Second, and less important, the listing of a new industrial consolidation often meant that the issues of the several firms entering the consolidation went off the list. The long-run increase in the number of issues listed was thus offset by the railroad and industrial consolidation issues of this period. Since the railroad reorganizations began in the early 1890's and industrial issues did not gain wide acceptance until 1897, it seems likely that the stock issues of industrial mergers were more the beneficiaries of the deepening of the market than its cause.

Among the outstanding stock market features of the period after 1897 was the increased sale of new industrial issues to the public,[14] hitherto sold principally by stockholder subscription. The post-1897 period was also noted for the development of the large-scale underwriting of industrial securities—a development not fully established, however, until after 1902. It is worth notice that the total volume of trading activity of 1901 was exceeded in only one year before 1919.

This description suggests that, by the late 1890's, the capital market had reached a sufficiently advanced stage of development to be capable of playing an important role in the merger movement. The quantitative and qualitative growth of the New York Stock Exchange from the early 1880's to the late 1890's was appreciable and was apparently based largely on factors other than the financing of mergers. With these developments at least tentatively established, an examination of certain aspects of the role of the capital market in the merger movement may proceed.

A rough demonstration of the degree to which merging firms employed the organized securities markets in marketing their securities issues can be made by determining the proportion of 1897–1902 consolidations whose stock appeared in the lists of securities traded on the New York Stock Exchange in the three

---

[13] See E. G. Campbell, *The Reorganization of the American Railroad System, 1893–1900*, Columbia University Press, 1938.

[14] Navin and Sears, *op. cit.*

years following the formation of each consolidation. Because case-by-case treatment of the disposition of stock issued by consolidations was impracticable, listing of a common or preferred stock on the New York Stock Exchange is here assumed to signify public trading activity for the stock. The share of the consolidations of the period of greatest merger activity, 1897–1902, whose stocks were traded on the New York Stock Exchange is presented by years in Table 50.

TABLE 50

Consolidations of 1897–1902 Whose Stocks Appeared on the New York Stock Exchange in the Three Years Following Consolidation

| | | | | | Capitalizations (millions of dollars) | | Percentage of Traded to All Consolidation Activity | | |
| | Consolidations | | Gross Disappearances | | | | | | |
Year	Traded	All	Traded	All	Traded	All	Consoli- dations	Dis- appear- ances	Capitali- zations
1897	2	9	27	73	70.0	110.9	22.2	37.0	63.1
1898	11	26	177	311	527.2	616.2	42.3	56.9	85.6
1899	31	106	529	1213	1333.3	2038.9	29.2	43.6	65.4
1900	3	43	20	338	81.0	382.7	6.1	5.9	21.2
1901	4	52	29	413	1471.0	1872.8	7.7	7.0	78.5
1902	5	49	29	315	188.5	689.1	10.2	9.2	27.4
Total	56	285	811	2663	3671.3	5710.6	19.6	30.5	64.3

Source: Worksheets and *The Commercial and Financial Chronicle, Investors Supplement*, 1900–1905.

The proportion was about one-fifth of all 1897–1902 consolidations, accounting for about one-third of gross firm disappearances and more than three-fifths of authorized capitalizations.

These consolidations were the larger ones of the period. The average capitalization of the consolidations traded on the New York Stock Exchange was $65.6 millions, while the average capitalization of consolidations not listed was $8.9 millions. The average gross firm disappearances into listed consolidations was 14.5 firms, while the average for nonlisted was 8.1 firms. Only 19.6 per cent of consolidations of all sizes were listed on the Exchange, whereas 64.8 per cent of consolidations capitalized at $20 million-and-over, and 78.6 per cent of $50 million-and-over consolidations, were listed.

When securities not listed on the New York Stock Exchange but listed on the Boston, Philadelphia, or Baltimore exchanges are included in the list, the proportion of 1897–1902 consolidations whose stocks were traded on the organized exchanges increases somewhat. The percentage for consolidations increases from 19.6

per cent to 23.2 per cent; that for gross firm disappearances from 30.5 per cent to 32.4 per cent; and that of consolidation capitalizations from 64.3 to 68.4 per cent.

These estimates of the proportion of consolidations that utilized the securities markets exclude those whose securities were traded on the unlisted markets and on the minor organized exchanges. By the very nature of the market, detailed statistics for such trading were not available. Some idea of the amount of unlisted and minor exchange trading is provided by the general quotation section of the *Commercial and Financial Chronicle, Investors Supplement,* which gives bid and asked quotations not only for securities of listed companies but also for unlisted and inactive stocks. A light sampling of this section uncovered a number of consolidations whose stocks were apparently traded in the minor exchanges or in the unlisted market. Therefore, the proportion of 1897–1902 consolidations using the major stock exchanges can be taken as a rough minimum limit of the proportion of consolidations whose securities were actively traded in the various securities markets.

From these findings we might infer that a substantial share of 1897–1902 consolidation activity resulted in the listing of securities on the organised securities markets. Without knowledge of how many consolidations used the stock exchanges directly to market their new security issues, it is still a reasonable conjecture that many of them found the organized exchanges either directly or indirectly helpful in raising capital. As anticipated, the issues of the more highly capitalized larger consolidations were listed more commonly than those of smaller consolidations.

Next to be examined is the importance of the sale of industrial securities to the general public for cash during the five-year period of high merger activity, 1898–1902. The findings will provide an indirect clue to the role of the securities markets of the period in selling new issues generally and, by inference, in marketing consolidation issues. The inferential error cannot be very grave because consolidation issues predominated among new securities issues of these years. The amount of common and preferred stock issues sold to the general public for cash can be compared with the amount of such issues exchanged for the tangible and intangible assets and the securities of other companies, including predecessor companies. In a period of high merger activity we should expect that the volume of stock exchanged for securities and assets of other companies would show a much greater degree of increase than the volume of stock sold to the general public for cash. If, instead, the relative increase proved greater for cash sales to the public, we might attach greater importance to such sales and to the organized exchanges, in feeding the merger boom.

Estimates of the amount of equity securities issued for public cash sale and to other companies for assets and securities are provided in *A Study of Saving in the United States*.[15] These two values are compared in Table 51 for the low merger year 1897, the high

TABLE 51

Comparison of Cash Sale of Industrial Common and Preferred Stock to General Public and Issue of Such Stock for Assets or Securities of Other Companies, 1897–1907

(amounts of stock in millions of dollars)

	Amount		Percentage			
Period	Cash issue to general public	Exchanged for assets or securities of other companies	Cash issue to general public	Exchanged for assets or securities of other companies	Amount issued for all purposes[a]	Percentage of two indicated purposes to all purposes
1897	4	62	6.0	94.0	138	47.8
1898–1902	360	3,026	10.6	89.4	6,205	54.6
1903–1907	28	285	8.8	91.2	447	70.0

a Includes (in addition to the indicated purposes) other cash issues, and stock issued to own shareholders for new money, or as stock dividends; and stock issued for acquisition or retirement of own securities. Some of total stock issued was classified as unissued, unsold, or disposition unknown.

Source: Raymond W. Goldsmith, *A Study of Saving in the United States*, Vol. I, Tables V-23 and V-24, pp. 503–505.

merger years 1898–1902, and the low merger years 1903–1907. The comparisons indicate that, as merger activity increased, volume of stock sold to the public for cash rose relatively more than that of stock exchanged for other companies' assets or securities. Also, the public sale of stock declined relatively more as merger activity waned.

These findings provide positive though not decisive support for the theory that the development of a large-scale capital market was necessary to support the merger movement. A well-developed market might be essential even though none of the new security issues was sold to the public for cash. The ability to readily "cash in" securities received in exchange for assets of merged firms would have been an important factor in persuading entrepreneurs to join consolidations. Without well-developed securities exchanges, un-

[15] Raymond W. Goldsmith, *A Study of Saving in the United States*, 3 vols., Princeton University Press, 1955 and 1956.

certainty about the ability to realize cash for consolidation securities might have precluded widespread consolidation activity. Another way of testing indirectly the theory that development of the capital stock market was a factor in the timing of the large merger wave and in merger activity in general is by comparing changes in merger activity with changes in stock prices. Two measures of merger activity—net firm disappearances by merger, and adjusted merger capitalizations—have been correlated with the industrial stock price index, and with the industrial production index. The production index was introduced into the analysis on the assumption that the level of industrial activity is an important factor in mergers. If differences between the effects of industrial activity and of stock prices on mergers appear, they may help to reveal the influence of stock prices.

Quarterly series for mergers, stock prices, and industrial production were obtained for the period 1895–1904, which encompassed the huge turn-of-the-century merger wave. Table 52 gives

TABLE 52

Coefficients of Correlation of Merger Activity with Stock Prices and Industrial Production by Quarters, 1895–1904

| | Measure of Merger Activity | |
	Firm disappearances	Capitalization
Coefficients of Simple Correlation between—		
Mergers and stock prices	+0.613	+0.536
Mergers and industrial production	+0.259	+0.179
Coefficients of partial correlation between—		
Mergers and stock prices after allowing for changes in industrial production	+0.608	+0.564
Mergers and industrial production after allowing for changes in stock prices	−0.243	−0.274

Source: Quarterly data, Tables B-1, B-2, and C-7.

the results of correlating each of the two measures of merger activity with stock prices and industrial production. Partial correlation analysis was also employed, as the intercorrelation between stock prices and industrial production was sufficiently high (+0.659) to make the simple correlation coefficients somewhat misleading.[16]

[16] The coefficients of simple and partial correlation between mergers and stock prices are significantly greater than zero at the 1 per cent level of significance for both measures of merger activity. Neither the simple nor partial correlation coefficients between mergers and industrial production depart significantly from zero, with use of the 5 per cent level of significance, for either measure of merger activity.

Merger activity exhibits a moderate positive relationship to stock price changes both before and after allowing for production level changes. This is true of both measures of merger activity in roughly the same degree. These correlations were obtained using unsmoothed merger data, which were subject to sharp interquarter irregular variations; with smoothed merger data, the correlations would be higher.

The relationship of merger activity to changes in industrial production is much lower than its relationship to stock price changes. The positive simple correlation coefficients and negative partial coefficients suggest that the changes in stock prices were responsible for the positive simple correlation between mergers and industrial production. When the effects of stock price changes are removed by partial correlation the "pure" relationship between industrial production and mergers becomes slightly negative. Since merger activity generally tends to follow business conditions rather than to move opposite to them, this finding suggests that, in years of peak merger activity, movements in stock prices may be more important than those in industrial production.[17]

STOCK MARKET EXPERIENCE OF LARGE CONSOLIDATIONS

Much of the debate over the desirability and consequences of the early merger wave has turned around the financial success of the large mergers of the period. Arthur Stone Dewing argued that "the trusts turned out ill," while Shaw Livermore argued that Dewing's findings needed reappraisal. Dewing compared the earnings of thirty-five prominent consolidations in the ten years following the merger with the earnings of the constituent companies before the merger, and with the promoters' estimates of prospective earnings. He concluded that the consolidations as a whole were not particularly successful.[18] Livermore traced the earnings records of 328 mergers until 1932 and concluded that the proportion that were successful was large enough to raise a serious question about Dewing's findings.[19]

An important aspect of the financial experience of these early mergers, not examined in either of the two studies, is the dividend record and market-price experience of their common stock. Com-

17 The experience in the late 1920's also tends to support this hypothesis. Stock prices rose 150 per cent from 1926 to 1929, merger activity rose 165 per cent, and industrial production rose only 25 per cent.

18 Arthur S. Dewing, "Statistical Test of the Success of Consolidations," *Quarterly Journal of Economics*, November 1921, pp. 84–101.

19 Shaw Livermore, "The Success of Industrial Mergers," *Quarterly Journal of Economics*, November 1935, pp. 68–96.

mon stock, unlike senior issues, carried no guarantee of dividends or interest. It was commonly issued in payment for the goodwill of the acquired companies, whereas bonds and preferred stock were issued for tangible assets. The behavior of the common stock, therefore, might indicate more accurately the degree to which organizers of mergers erected sound financial structures and succeeded in obtaining profitable control of their markets.

Therefore, an examination of the dividend and market-price records of the common stock of thirteen large 1899 or 1901 consolidations was undertaken.[20] The market price of the stock of each was recorded on the first market day in December of the year of the consolidation. As most of them were organized in the first half of the year, the observation date is five to ten months after the organization—sufficient time for the stock to have been "seasoned" in the market and for the promoters to have played their role and left the market. A nine-year interval was chosen for tracing the dividend records of the consolidations; that is, a medium-run period, with terminal dates of December 1908 and December 1910 at which the industrial stock price index was neither at a peak nor a trough. The stock was assumed to have been sold on December 21 of either 1908 or 1910. Crude rates of return were computed, representing the compound-interest growth in the value of the stock over the period. The dividends received were included in the growth, but were assumed to be not reinvested. The reinvestment assumption would have entailed a detailed investigation of market prices throughout the period and numerous other more complicated computations, which because of the relative shortness of the period would have increased the rate of return very little.

The market records of the common stocks of the thirteen large consolidations are presented in Table 53.

If an individual had invested the same amount of money in each of the thirteen stocks, his return on his investment over this hybrid nine-year period would have been 5.9 per cent. If he had invested an amount in each of the thirteen stocks proportional to the size of its authorized capitalization his return would have been 7.4 per cent. This would not have been much better than the 7 per cent dividend commonly offered on the industrial preferred issues of this period and the 5 per cent nominal interest rate on industrial bonds. However, it contrasts favorably with the yields on railroad bonds of 3.9 per cent in December 1899 and 3.7 per cent in

[20] Selection of the thirteen consolidations focused on the need for wide industrial representation in the sample as well as on highly capitalized firms whose securities had public sale and continuous price records in the financial journals.

December 1901. Railroad bonds were the only securities for which true yield data could be found.

Thus, on the average, the common-stock investor realized a positive though not very large return on his investment in the nine-year period following the merger, a period which spanned two serious

TABLE 53

Nine-Year Market Experience of Common Stocks of Thirteen Large 1899 and 1901 Consolidations

Company	Date of Organi- zation	Market Price Dec. 1 (2) of Organi- zation Year	Market Price Dec. 21 9 years later	Dividends Received	Crude Average Annual Percentage Rate of Return
United Shoe Machinery	2/7/99	$33.00	$178.91	$29.34	+22.7
American Car & Foundry	2/20/99	16.75	45.25	16.00	+15.5
American Smelting & Refining	4/4/99	40.25	79.00	31.25	+11.9
U.S. Steel	4/1/01	43.50	72.63	21.75	+9.0
American Locomotive	6/10/01	31.13	36.00	10.00	+4.4
American Woolen	3/29/99	22.00	28.00	0.00	+2.7
Distilling Co. of America	7/12/99	8.50	5.95	4.12	+1.9
Republic Iron & Steel	5/3/99	25.38	24.00	0.00	−0.6
American Can	3/19/01	16.25	9.00	0.00	−6.4
Allis-Chalmers	5/7/01	20.50	8.13	0.00	−7.8
American Ice	3/11/99	34.13	4.65	9.00	−9.7
Union Bag & Paper	2/27/99	25.50	9.25	0.00	−10.7
U.S. Cotton Duck	6/4/01	20.50	4.60	0.00	−15.3
Geometric average of rates of return:					
Simple					+5.9
Weighted[a]					+7.4
Railroad bond yields:[b]					
Dec. 1899					+3.9
Dec. 1901					+3.7

[a] Weighted by size of authorized capitalization.

[b] Frederick R. Macaulay, *Some Theoretical Problems Suggested by the Movements of Interest Rates, Bond Yields and Stock Prices in the United States since 1856*, National Bureau of Economic Research, 1938.

Source: Moody's Manuals and *Commercial and Financial Chronical*, for appropriate years.

crises in the stock market and a major business depression. Further, common stock was junior to usually heavy issues of 7 per cent cumulative preferred stock and 5 per cent bonds. That seven of the thirteen common stocks paid dividends, and seven of the thirteen offered a positive return on the investment over this period indicates that the promise to investors of increasing equity value was at least partly realized in a fair share of cases.

The almost equal number with unsatisfactory market records suggests, on the other hand, that a good fraction of the consolidations did not bear out this promise. Possibly the proportion of unsatisfactory outcomes corresponds to the risks promoters were willing to take. Yet, in the optimism of the years of peak merger activity, the risk of failure must have looked very small to promoters.

These findings, on balance, probably weaken the argument that the consolidation movement was due exclusively to the desire of promoters for high, quick-turnover profits to the neglect of sound financial principles. One need only recall the personal dislike of the conservative promoter J. P. Morgan for the speculative promoter "Bet-a-Million" Gates to illustrate the diversity of motives and techniques among the organizers of early mergers. It seems unlikely, for example, that Morgan, who had just spent a decade trying to produce order in the financial structures of railroads, would zealously participate in the gross overcapitalization of industrial mergers. The statistical test remains inconclusive. The market dominance achieved by many of these consolidations may have permitted profits sufficiently large to cover their high-interest and preferred-dividend commitments—fixed obligations that would have caused trouble to consolidations failing to secure strong market positions.

CONCLUSION

The organized securities market had experienced important and substantial growth in the last quarter of the nineteenth century, probably as a concomitant of the general economic growth of the country, and was therefore large enough to support the huge turn-of-the-century merger wave. The market's immediate relationship to the merger movement was complex; changes in the capital market permitted developments in merger activity which, in turn, caused further changes in the capital market. However, in view of the earlier and important role played by railroad reorganizations in these changes in the capital market, industrial mergers were probably more the beneficiaries of the changes in the capital market than a cause of them.

A large fraction of the larger and more important 1897–1902 consolidations listed their stock on the organized securities exchanges where it entered into trading activity. Moreover, industrial securities sold for cash to the general public became a relatively larger part of new securities issues during the large merger wave.

A correlation analysis of merger activity and stock-price changes, using industrial production as a control variable, indicated that in this period of peak merger activity mergers were more closely related to stock-price changes than to industrial activity changes. Indeed, though mergers are probably related positively to long-run movements in industrial production, in this period the effect of stock-price changes apparently overrode the immediate influence of industrial production.

The market experience of the stocks of a small sample of consolidations suggests that investors in the common stocks of the leading consolidations fared not much worse than holders of preferred stock and perhaps a little better than bondholders. So far as it goes, this finding lends no support to either of the extreme views —that common stock of mergers was an investment success, or that it was merely a device for exploiting gullible investors.

The British merger movement also paralleled more closely changes in stock prices than changes in industrial production (see Appendix A). Since the greatest growth in the British capital market probably occurred much earlier than that in the United States, it is not a development that can be designated as an immediate cause of the British merger wave very late in the nineteenth century. Developments in business organization may be relevant here. Not until the 1880's in England were the full potentialities of limited liability realized in corporate practice (though legally prepared for much earlier): what was achieved quickly in the United States was achieved gradually in Great Britain. A convergence of unrestricted corporate behavior and large capital markets may have been important in setting the stage for mergers, and may help explain the almost simultaneous occurrence of great merger waves in the two countries, at the turn of the century.

The Market Control Motive

A frequent explanation for the merger movement is that mergers represented attempts on the part of businessmen and financiers to achieve market control.[21] One cannot measure the market control motive directly. As one of the many manifestations of the profit motive, market control may be substituted for by other profit-increasing conditions. Moreover, it is inextricably tied up with

[21] See, for example, Joe S. Bain, in *The Growth of the American Economy*, 2nd ed., H. F. Williamson, ed., Prentice-Hall, 1951, Chap. 32; and Hans B. Thorelli, *The Federal Antitrust Policy, Origin of an American Tradition*, Johns Hopkins Press, 1955, p. 280.

external economic forces on the entrepreneur.[22] Lacking direct observation of the motive, we may study its effects. By examining the results of the merger wave in terms of market control achieved we may be able to make inferences about the importance of the desire for such control.

EVIDENCE OF MARKET CONTROL

The data describing the degree of market control achieved by the major mergers of the 1895–1904 period are taken from *The Truth About The Trusts*.[23] In this book Moody estimated the share of the industry controlled by each of ninety-two important trusts. No attempt was made to construct independent estimates of shares of markets controlled, either for the trusts listed by Moody or for those he did not list, with the following exception. Two industries in which a high degree of local market control was the characteristic result of the merger have been added to Moody's list—breweries and ice companies. They were assigned to a percentage-controlled category designated "large." It should be added that Moody used this qualitative designation for a number of industries, where the apparent industry control was substantially more than 50 per cent.

If we assume that the Moody estimates individually are reasonably accurate, then our estimates of the proportion of merger activity resulting in market dominance can be regarded as minimum estimates. A considerable number of mergers not included by Moody probably achieved a high degree of control in local or regional markets, where the computations of exact percentages were not possible.

The number of consolidations achieving given degrees of market control presented below do not exactly correspond to those presented in Moody, for two reasons. First, the present writer adopted different class intervals than Moody's, in order to center the more common percentages within the class interval. Second, Moody listed a number of nonmanufacturing or nonmining mergers, and of pre-1895 trusts, which have been excluded because not covered by the merger data of this study. One major trust, Standard Oil, was left out because almost all of its merging activity took place well before 1896.

Certain adjustments were required in the totals for numbers of

---

[22] A common explanation of the "increased desire for market control" in certain industries in the 1890's was the downward pressure on prices caused by what was thought to be declining demand for the product, aggravated by too much productive capacity.

[23] John Moody, *The Truth About The Trusts*, Moody, 1904.

consolidations, firm disappearances, and capitalizations. Earlier consolidations entering into later consolidations were deducted from the totals, both for number and capitalizations of mergers; only the capitalization of the last consolidation in the period was included.[24] But firms absorbed by earlier consolidations later absorbed by further consolidations were included in the disappearances total. In industries in which acquisition was the dominant form of merger, the capitalization of the latest incorporation of the parent company was included in the capitalization totals, to make these mergers comparable to consolidations in this dimension of size.

The distribution of merger activity in industries in which market dominance was achieved is presented in Table 54. It is

TABLE 54

Proportion of Merger Activity Accounted for by Merged Firms That
Achieved Market Control, 1895–1904

Percentage of Industry Controlled	Consolidations and Parent Companies		Firm Disappearances		Capitalizations (millions of dollars)	
	Number	Per cent of total	Number	Per cent of total	Value	Per cent of total
42.5–62.5	21	6.7	291	9.7	613.5	10.3
62.5–82.5	24	7.7	529	17.6	2,130.6	35.7
82.5-over	16	5.1	343	11.4	998.0	16.7
"Large"	25	8.0	302	10.0	455.5	7.6
	86	27.5	1,465	48.6	4,197.6	70.4
Total merger activity	313	100.0	3,012	100.0	5,960.9	100.0

Source: See accompanying text.

evident that a substantial share of total 1895–1904 merger activity did result in securing a leading and often dominant share of the market. Almost one-half of firm disappearances, and seven-tenths of merger capitalizations were accounted for by mergers that gained a leading position in the market. Considering that these are minimum estimates, it might not be too misleading to place the actual share of disappearances into market-leading firms as high as two-thirds of all merger disappearances, and the share of such firms' capitalizations as high as three-fourths or four-fifths of all merger capitalizations.

[24] For a list of major consolidations subsequently entering larger consolidations, see Table C-6.

CONCLUSION

Whatever the precise share of merger activity resulting in the control of markets, the above evidence shows that it was substantial. As we have noted, it would be extremely shaky reasoning to attribute this high "monopolization" activity to a fundamental increase in businessmen's desire for market control. But the findings do warrant certain inferences. First, they tend to demonstrate the existence of a fairly strong desire to avoid rigorous competition. Second, if we assume that the promoter and financier were important motive forces in the merger movement, it seems probable that the promise of "monopoly" profits would have served as one of the more effective inducements for firms to surrender their independence.

Note on Economies of Scale

Technological revolution leading to great economies of production in large-scale enterprises has been regarded by many merger students as of transcendent importance. Examination of this factor is not feasible, largely because the data on mergers lack sufficient detail for an assessment of scale economies on an individual merger basis. A few observations of certain aspects of the phenomenon may be in order, however, for indirect light on its importance in the early merger movement.

In scanning the basic data gathered in this study, one is struck by the overwhelming share of merger activity made up of what appear to be horizontal mergers. The vertical merger was characteristically found in the primary metals industries, but appeared only infrequently in the great variety of other industries having large merger activity. This suggests that the economies of vertical integration, upon which many merger students have placed great stress, played a relatively small role in the merger movement.

Another feature of the merger movement is the great diversity in types of production operations among the industries in which mergers occurred. The description of the industrial composition of the merger movement presented in Chapter 3 demonstrated that variety. It is hard to believe that such a variety of technological developments as would be needed to bring production economies of scale to these diverse industries could have converged in the same short period of time.

In the present chapter, the joint contribution of the capital market and the promoter in the creation of firms controlling major shares of their markets emerges as an important factor. It may have overridden other developments that presumably might have exerted an influence on merger activity. Emphasis on the control of markets might well have been more important than cost factors in determining firm size. It would be difficult to demonstrate that the most efficient or potentially most efficient firm size from the cost standpoint was systematically related to the size of the market —as would have to be demonstrated if scale economies were to be reconciled with market control.[25]

Lacking more complete data with which to test the reasoning, however, this discussion of scale economies must remain conjectural.

Summary and Conclusions

We have examined four historical developments that have been prominent among the explanations of the early merger movement. Other common explanations could not be tested, notably economies of scale, for want of adequate data. Even although the examination is incomplete, the detailed tests of the several hypotheses serve to place the merger wave in clearer perspective.

The findings concerning the role of industry growth retardation in the early merger movement raise a serious question as to the validity of that hypothesis. The years preceding the merger wave saw a reversal of the pattern of retardation, especially in the very industries where merger activity was highest. The observed pattern of industry growth acceleration could hardly be credited with causing the kind of increased competitive pressure on business firms that the retardation hypothesis alleged. Indeed, we would expect that acceleration of market growth would cause a relaxation of competitive pressures, and thus a diminution of the impetus toward merging.

The transportation system underwent a large and protracted expansion in the decades preceding the merger wave. The effect of this development on merger activity is hard to assess, however. It probably did place geographically separated firms in more direct competition with one another. On the other hand, mergers occurred more commonly in industries that were geographically concentrated than in those more widely dispersed. Furthermore, the

[25] Stigler (*op. cit.*, p. 29) found that the near-monopolies created at the turn of the century almost invariably experienced a substantial decline in market share as time passed.

growth of transportation was accompanied by, and was probably a partial cause of, acceleration in market growth, which permitted a firm to pursue a more independent course. The period was also characterized by substantial increases in the tariff, protecting domestic industries from international competition. In view of these offsetting factors it seems unlikely that transportation growth could be accounted a major cause of the merger movement.

The findings concerning the role of the capital market in the merger movement lend considerable support to the thesis that the development of the capital market was a major cause. The high correlation between merger activity and stock prices suggests that much of the merger activity of the period had its origin in, or was influenced by, the stock market. Further examination indicated that capital market factors overrode the level of industrial activity in influencing merger activity. This suggests that cost-price relationships in business firms were a less important influence than many students believed.

The desire for market control probably played at least a permissive role in the merger movement. The large proportion of merger activity resulting in market control suggests that the desire for the protection thus afforded to profits must have been a factor of substantial importance in inducing firms to merge. With the growth of the capital market this desire found an effective means of implementation. Coupled with the expectation of gains to be reaped from a rising stock market, the added promise of protected profits must have represented a compelling argument for independent firms to join into consolidations.

Chapter 5. Merger Movements and Business Cycles, 1895–1956

In the preceding chapter we tested theories of the first merger wave set in the context of historical development, passing over the role of short-run cyclical changes. It was apparent, however, that the business cycle was important in the timing of the first merger movement. Revival of merger activity did not occur until the depressed conditions of the mid-1890's had passed and the prosperous turn-of-the-century years were reached. Also, the merger expansion occurred during a cyclically rising stock market. The infrequency of merger movements indicates that they have not sprung up with every business expansion. However there are several ways in which merger activity might be expected to respond to business cycles.

The acquisition of one firm by another or the consolidation of several firms into one is an act of investment by the initiator of the merger, in many respects the same as other forms of investment. The calculation made by the entrepreneur in balancing the cost of the to-be-acquired firms with the future earnings ability of the merged firm is the same type of calculation he makes in deciding to build another plant, or to organize a new business. Merger activity, viewed as a form of private investment, might be expected to respond, as private investment has been shown by various studies to respond, in a positive and sensitive fashion to the business cycle.[1]

A merger may represent more than an act of pure investment, however. The merged firm may gain greater control over its market and enhanced ability to raise prices, control production, and otherwise exploit the market. The profits of such market control are of course all the greater if the market is expanding. We might thus expect attempts at mergers for market control to occur early in a cyclical expansion, when expectations become favorable. The expectations of the prospective acquirees would also become favorable,[2] however, and their unwillingness to sell out at a sufficiently

[1] For a summary of the sensitivity and conformity of investment activity to the business cycle, see Wesley C. Mitchell, *What Happens During Business Cycles: A Progress Report*, National Bureau of Economic Research, 1951, Table 16, Sections B, C, D, pp. 161–163.

[2] Theoretically the acquiree could hold out for a price that would represent a little less than the discounted value of the difference in the profits of the merged and unmerged acquirer. Moreover, if the would-be acquirer is a leading firm in the industry, the acquiree might decide it would be more profitable to stay out of the merger, and let the big firm set a "monopoly" price at which the small firm could sell all of his output, rather than his pro-rata share of the monopoly output of the merged firm. See George J. Stigler, "Monopoly and Oligopoly by Merger," *Papers and Proceedings of the American Economic Association*, May 1950, pp. 23–25.

low price might prevent such mergers. The desire for merger may be less urgent if the various firms are operating at less than full capacity, and independent, immediate, and profitable expansion may be possible. The merger may be accomplished only when the expansion of the various firms has proceeded to a point at which they are operating at capacity. The opportunity for immediate increase in capacity, coupled with the advantages of market control, may cause the initiator of the merger to offer a premium price to a solicited firm. Such firms may also have reached a receptive mood, if profits can no longer be increased quickly through internal expansion. We might thus expect to find merger activity occurring at the stage in a cyclical expansion when many industries have reached capacity production.

The condition of the capital market may also affect the ·time pattern of mergers. Firms expanding by merger, as in other forms of firm growth, frequently turn to public sources for the needed extra funds. New capital issues are most common when the acquired firms are purchased for cash; but when the purchase is made by exchange of stock, new securities are frequently issued to increase working capital. Even when a pure stock-for-stock transaction is made, the organizers of the merger are sensitive to the recent trend of the stock market, because ratios of exchange are partly determined by the market prices of the securities of the merging firms. We might expect to find mergers occurring—as with other aspects of corporate financing—when the recent history of stock prices has indicated a strong tendency toward further increase. This is usually some time after the initial faltering stages of stock price recovery, and during a time when the market has exhibited a sustained upward movement. As the end of the expansion is ordinarily not anticipated, merges may occur when stock prices are on the verge of moving downward.

The interval required to conceive, plan, and execute a merger is a complicating factor in the response of mergers to the business cycle. Whether this time lag is longer than that found in the ordinary investment action is open to question. Unlike an ordinary act of investment, the merger requires initial steps that are likely to be complex and time consuming. Permission may have to be obtained from stockholders, minority objections settled, and authorization for corporate charter changes obtained from state commissions or courts. Once arranged, however, the transfer of control may be carried out rapidly, for the "new plant" is already a fully operating business. The construction of a new plant—a type of investment that is quickly arranged—may take a considerable period of time. If future earnings expectations are assumed to be calculated from the date the enlarged facilities go into operation, the time response of merger "investment spending" may be actually shorter than that of ordinary investment spending.

In the light of the interplay of these factors and circumstances, we might expect to find merger activity at its highest in the expansion phase of the business cycle. The peak of merger activity is not likely to occur very early in the expansion, but just how far the expansion must advance before the merger peak is reached is not clear. Since stock market conditions reflect general business expectations,[3] and in turn directly affect the launching of mergers, it seems likely that the response of merger activity to economic conditions would resemble the response of new business formation. Merger activity thus might correspond quite closely to changes in the number of business incorporations.

With the new 1895-1920 series of mergers and the comprehensive series dating from 1919 through 1954, the stage is set for examining the behavior of merger activity over a number of cycles of business activity. This six-decade period encompasses all the large waves and all but one of the minor flurries of merger activity in manufacturing and mining. A minor merger wave occurred in 1888-1892, but it was so small that its exclusion will not seriously weaken the tests.

The successive sections of the various merger series, though differing from one another in a number of ways, have one measure of merger activity common to all—the number of firm disappearances by merger. Accordingly, this is the measure used in the analyses below. A visual comparison of merger disappearances and the business cycle is presented in Chart 5. The chart also contains quarterly series of industrial production and stock prices to be used later in the chapter.[4]

The merger activity of the past six decades has exhibited high, though not perfect, conformity to changes in general business conditions (Table 55). The National Bureau of Economic Research has recorded fourteen cycles in general business activity between 1897 and 1954. The series of merger disappearances exhibited twelve cycles of activity.[5] Eleven of the twelve merger cycles showed

---

[3] For a discussion of the relationship between expectations and stock prices, see "An Appraisal of Data and Research on Businessmen's Expectation," *Report of Consultant Committee on General Business Expectations to the Board of Governors of the Federal Reserve System*, Joint Committee of the Economic Report, September 1955, pp. 119-128.

[4] For a detailed description of the various merger series, see Chapter 3.

[5] I am indebted to Victor Zarnowitz of the National Bureau for much thoughtful advice on the treatment of the cyclical relationships.

TABLE 55

Relationship between Reference Cycles and Merger Cycles, 1897–1954

Turning Point	Quarter Year		Merger Cycle Lead (−) or Lag (+) in Quarters	Rank in Amplitude and Duration			
				Fourteen reference cycle expansions		Fourteen reference cycle contractions	
	Reference cycle	Merger cycle		Amplitude	Duration	Amplitude	Duration
Trough	II '97	III '96	−3				
Peak	III '99	III '99	0	5	7		
Trough	IV '00	II '00	−2			10.5	7.5
Peak	IV '02	IV '01	−4	13	8.5		
Trough	III '04	III '04	0			10.5	3
Peak	II '07	III '05	−7	8	6		
Trough	II '08	I '09	+3			5	11
Peak	I '10	I '10	0	6	10.5		
Trough	IV '11					13	3
Peak	I '13			14	13		
Trough	IV '14	II '14	−2			6	3
Peak	III '18	I '17	−6	4	3		
Trough	II '19	IV '18	−2			7	13.5
Peak	I '20	I '20 II ('20)a	0 (+1)	9	14		
Trough	III '21					4	5
Peak	II '23			3	10.5		
Trough	III '24	III '23	−4			8	7.5
Peak	III '26	I '26	−2	10	8.5		
Trough	IV '27	I '27	−3			14	7.5
Peak	II '29	I '29	−1	11	12		
Trough	I '33	IV '33	+3			1	1
Peak	II '37	I '36	−5	2	2		
Trough	II '38	III '39	+5			2	11
Peak		II '40		1	1		
Trough		III '42					
Peak	I '45	II '44	−3				
Trough	IV '45	II '45	−2			3	13.5
Peak	IV '48	II '46	−10	12	5		
Trough	IV '49	II '49	−2			9	11
Peak	II '53			7	4		
Trough	III '54					12	7.5

TIMING SEQUENCE, MERGER CYCLES RELATIVE TO REFERENCE CYCLES

	Peaks	Troughs
Number of leads	8	8
Number of coincidences	2	1
Number of lags	1	3
Average lead (−) or lag (+) in quarters	−3.4	−0.8

a Figures in parentheses show second segment of the series, included in count and averages.

Source: Reference cycle chronology for 1897–1919 is from Geoffrey H. Moore, *Statistical Indicators of Cyclical Revivals and Recessions*, Occasional Paper 31, National Bureau of Economic Research, 1950, p. 6, Table 1; for later years from Standard Reference Dates for Business Cycles, United States, 1919–1954 (NBER, mimeographed)

Merger turning points were dated by the business cycle staff of the NBER. The merger series was deseasonalized in the UNIVAC program, and the deseasonalized series was used in dating the turning points. Amplitude measures were derived from NBER worksheets, and were based on the American Telephone and Telegraph, Persons, and Ayres indexes of business cycles. A low rank number signifies that the given expansion or contraction was among the largest in amplitude among the fourteen expansions or contractions of the period.

CHART 5

Quarterly Series of Firm Disappearances by Merger, Industrial Stock Price Index, and Industrial Production Index, 1895–1955

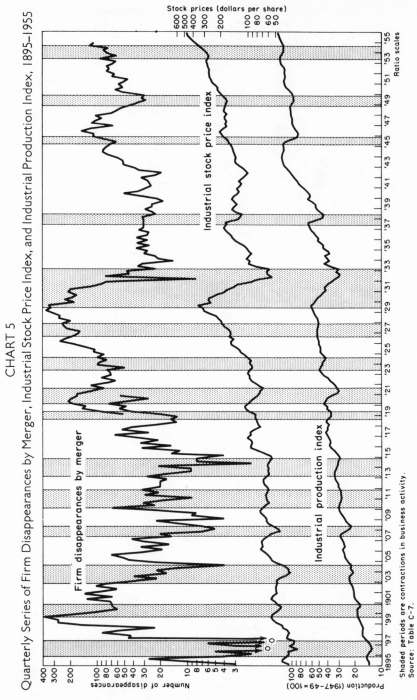

Stock prices (dollars per share)

Industrial stock price index

Firm disappearances by merger

Industrial production index

Number of disappearances

Production (1947–49 = 100)

Shaded periods are contractions in business activity.

Source: Table C-7.

Ratio scales

a definite timing relationship to the turning points of reference cycles.

The reference cycle phases skipped over by the merger series were usually either of short duration or of moderate amplitude. There were two reference expansions for which there was no corresponding merger expansion, 1911–1913 and 1921–1923. These were among the shortest of the fourteen reference cycle expansions of the period, and the 1911–1913 expansion was among the mildest of the reference expansions.

The expansion of 1921–1923 was vigorous, however, and it is not clear why merger activity did not respond. A possible explanation is the relative shortness of the expansion (7 quarters as against an average expansion period of 10.7 quarters). Another explanation might be that the sharp revival of industrial production was not matched by an equally sharp rise in stock prices (Chart 5). The absence of merger revival may thus signify that the rise in production might not have been accompanied by an equally strong increase in business optimism as reflected in stock prices.

There was one reference cycle contraction that had no corresponding merger contraction—1953–1954, one of the mildest contractions in the six-decade period. One merger contraction had no corresponding reference cycle contraction—that of 1940–1942. This downturn in mergers accompanied a downturn in stock prices, even though general business conditions and industrial production were expanding.[6]

The response of merger activity to business conditions from 1933 through 1945 suggests possible additional factors required for the revival of merger activity. The economic expansion of 1933–1937, while large and protracted, did not result in the restoration of the high production levels of the late 1920's, nor was there a substantial increase in merger activity. It was not until the greater expansion of 1938–1945, especially after the wartime expansion following 1941, that merger activity rose substantially above the low levels of the 1930's. This suggests that the reappearance of merger activity may require not simply a cyclical expansion but one that has attained a substantial recovery of employment and production.

Peaks of merger activity most commonly preceded the peaks of the reference cycle. The average merger lead for the eleven peaks common to both cycles was 3.4 quarters. The longest leads, with the exception of the 1901 secondary peak on the huge wave, occurred in times of generally low merger activity. The high merger peak of 1899 coincided with the reference cycle peak, while

6 See Table 56.

111

that of 1929 led the reference peak by only one quarter. Near-coincidence in timing also characterized the sharp, though lesser, peak of 1920. This suggests that the periods of extremely high merger activity may be more prolonged than periods of more restrained merger activity.

The time sequence for troughs was somewhat less consistent than that for peaks. Merger troughs preceded reference troughs, on the average, by only 0.8 quarters, and lagged them on three occasions. This irregular time sequence probably indicates that economic forces in a depression are likely to be diffuse and weak, compelling no great uniformity in the response of merger activity.

TIME SEQUENCE OF MERGER-RELATED CYCLES

The general business cycle is a composite of many economic series. The cyclical time pattern of each of the various series is to some degree unique, and the patterns differ, among other ways, in the timing of their turning points. For many series this timing pattern is consistently related to that of other series and to that of the general business cycle. Some series experience turning points that precede those of most other series, while others coincide with or follow the majority of turning points.

We shall examine the time sequence of the merger cycle relative to other cycles, to determine whether a consistent sequence exists between mergers and other presumably related series. Five series will be compared: the reference cycle; industrial stock prices; the volume of stock trading; business incorporations; and industrial production. They were chosen because of indications, discussed earlier, that they are representative of forces likely to be related to mergers, and because requisite data were available. Such factors as cycles in technological innovation and in industrial reorganization were not included because they were not reducible to quantitative form.

The turning points in the merger series were in quarterly form. For use with the other series, they were converted into monthly form by taking as the turning point the center month of the appropriate quarter. The monthly turning points for merger activity and related series are shown in Table 56.

Comparison of the turning point dates of the reference cycle and of cycles in specific series suggests a consistent sequence of events (Table 57). The pattern is different for peaks and troughs. In expansions the peak in stock trading is reached first, followed by merger activity, stock prices, business incorporations, the reference cycle, and industrial production, in that order. In contractions

112

TABLE 56

Cyclical Turning Points of Merger Series and Five Related Series, 1896–1954

			Month and Year of Turning Point			
	Merger cycle	Reference cycle	Industrial production	Stock prices	Stock trading	Incorporations
Trough	8/96	6/97	9/96	...	5/97	9/96
Peak	...	...	...	...	...	9/97
Trough	...	...	...	...	...	5/98
Peak	8/99	6/99	2/00	9/99	1/99	7/99
Trough	5/00	12/00	10/00	9/10	8/00	2/00
Peak	11/01	9/02	7/03	6/01	5/01	5/01
Trough	...	...	...	...	...	9/01
Peak	...	...	...	...	...	2/03
Trough	8/04	8/04	12/03	11/03	5/04	4/04
Peak	8/05	5/07	5/07	1/06	1/06	1/07
Trough	2/09	6/08	5/08	11/07	11/07	12/07
Peak	2/10	1/10	3/10	11/09	6/09	11/09
Trough	...	1/12	1/11	7/10	4/11	7/10
Peak	...	1/13	1/13	9/12	9/11	7/12
Trough	5/14	12/14	11/14	12/14	12/14	12/14
Peak	2/17	8/18	5/17	11/16	9/16	1/17
Trough	11/18	4/19	3/19	12/17	4/18	11/18 (9/18)ᵃ
Peak	2/20 (5/20)	1/20	2/20	10/19	7/19	12/19
Trough	...	7/21	7/21	8/21	10/21	1/21
Peak	...	5/23	6/23	3/23	2/23	4/23
Trough	8/23	7/24	7/24	10/23	10/23	8/24 (6/24)
Peak	2/26	10/26	3/27	...	11/25	10/25
Trough	2/27	11/27	11/27	...	5/26	12/26
Peak	2/29	6/29	8/29	9/29	10/29	1/29
Trough	11/33	3/33	7/32	6/32	3/33	...
Peak	...	...	...	2/34	7/33	...
Trough	...	...	...	9/34	3/35	12/34 (12/34)
Peak	2/36	5/37	7/37	2/37	2/36	12/36
Trough	8/39	6/38	5/38	4/38	...	9/39
Peak	5/40	...	...	10/39	...	4/40
Trough	5/42	...	...	4/42	5/42	5/42
Peak	5/44	2/45	11/43	5/46	...	4/46
Trough	5/45	10/45	2/46	...	...	...
Peak	5/46	11/48	10/48	...	1/46	...
Trough	5/49	10/49	10/49	6/49	1/49	4/49
Peak	...	7/53	7/53	1/53	1/51	5/50
Trough	...	8/54	8/54	9/53	8/52	6/51

ᵃ Dates in parentheses are beginning turning points in the more recent of overlapping series, and are used in making timing comparisons.

Sources: Turning-point dates of reference cycle, stock prices, and stock trading were taken from business cycle files of the National Bureau of Economic Research. Industrial production series used are the Babson index from 1896 to 1917, and the Federal Reserve Board index from 1919 to 1954, both deseasonalized, and dated by the NBER. Incorporations turning points for 1896–1940 were taken from George H. Evans, Jr., *Business Incorporations in the United States, 1800–1943*, National Bureau of Economic Research, 1948, p. 85, Table 41; for 1942–1951 the turning points are those of Dun's series for forty-eight states. The merger series was deseasonalized and dated by the NBER business cycle unit; this quarterly series was converted to monthly by taking the center month of the turning point of the quarterly series as the monthly turning point.

113

TABLE 57

Timing of Turning Points in Merger Activity, Stock Trading, Stock Prices, Business Incorporations, and Industrial Production, Compared with the Reference Cycle, 1899–1949

Series	Average Lead (−) or Lag (+), Months		Average Deviation of Leads and Lags	
	Peaks	Troughs	Peaks	Troughs
Number of shares sold, New York Stock Exchange	− 10.5	− 6.3	7.0	3.4
Merger activity	− 7.6	− 3.9	8.4	4.5
Industrial stock prices (Dow Jones)	− 6.8	− 6.9	8.3	3.9
Business incorporations	− 5.6	− 4.6	4.4	2.5
Industrial production (FRB)	+ 1.3	− 1.9	4.4	1.8

Source: Table 56. There are eight peaks and seven troughs common to all of these series in the period 1899–1949.

the trough in stock prices is reached first, followed by stock trading, business incorporations, merger activity, industrial production, and the reference cycle. The implication is that in prosperity, merger activity tends to correspond most closely to capital market conditions, while in depression it corresponds most closely to industrial activity and general business conditions. This suggestion is confirmed by the correlation between merger activity, stock prices, and industrial production, presented later.

A simple ranking of turning points by order of occurrence alters the sequence somewhat from that indicated by the average leads in Table 57. As shown by Table 58, a simple average rank in order of sequence places the peak in stock trading first, followed by business incorporations, stock prices, merger activity, the reference cycle, and industrial production. In both Tables 57 and 58, however, peaks in merger activity bear a closer timing relationship to stock prices than to any other series. The sequence for cyclical troughs is essentially the same whether based upon average lags or upon average rank order of occurrence.

The merger series is directly compared in Table 59 to the three specific economic series that revealed the closest timing relationship to mergers in the reference cycle comparison—stock trading, stock prices, and business incorporations. As the comparison shows, all three series are closely related to the merger series at both peaks and troughs, the average lag or lead in no instance being more than 2.9 months.

Merger activity exhibits the closest average lag or lead to stock prices at peaks, and to business incorporations at troughs. Con-

TABLE 58

Sequence of Cyclical Turning Points in Merger Activity, Stock Prices, Stock Trading, Business Incorporations, Industrial Production, and the Reference Cycle 1899-1949

Reference Cycle Turning Point	Rank in Order of Sequence					
	Stock trading	Stock prices	Business incorpora- tions	Merger activity	Industrial production	Reference cycle
Peaks:						
6/99	1	5	3	4	6	2
9/02	1.5	3	1.5	4	6	5
5/07	2.5	2.5	4	1	6	5
1/10	1	2.5	2.5	5	6	4
8/18	1	2	3	4	5	6
1/20	1	2	3	6	5	4
6/29	6	5	1	2	4	3
5/37	1.5	4	3	1.5	6	5
Troughs						
12/00	3	4	1	2	5	6
8/04	4	1	3	5.5	2	5.5
6/08	1.5	1.5	3	6	4	5
12/14	4.5	4.5	4.5	1	2	4.5
4/19	2	1	3	4	5	6
7/24	2.5	2.5	4	1	5.5	5.5
10/49	1	4	2	3	5.5	5.5
			AVERAGE RANK			
Peaks	1.9	3.3	2.6	3.4	5.5	4.3
Troughs	2.6	2.6	2.9	3.2	4.1	4.6

Source: Table 56.

TABLE 59

Timing of Cyclical Turning Points in Stock Trading, Stock Prices, and Business Incorporations Compared with Merger Activity 1899-1949

Series	Average Lead (−) or Lag (+), Months		Average Deviation of Leads and Lags	
	Peaks	Troughs	Peaks	Troughs
Number of shares sold, New York Stock Exchange	−2.9	−2.4	5.4	5.5
Industrial stock prices (Dow Jones)	+0.9	−2.7	5.4	6.3
Business incorporations	+1.3	−0.4	6.2	5.8
Average	−0.2	−1.8	5.7	5.9

Source: Table 56.

versely, the average deviation of lag or lead is greatest for incorporations at peaks, and for stock prices at troughs. Thus stock prices appear to be the most consistent immediate factor at merger peaks, while business incorporations are the most consistent immediate factor at merger troughs. Stock trading consistently leads merger activity at both peaks and troughs.

The relationship of merger activity to the three economic series is somewhat higher at peaks than at troughs. The over-all average lag or lead of the three series is smaller at peaks than at troughs; also, the over-all average deviation of lag or lead is slightly smaller at peaks than at troughs. This suggests that mergers more closely paralleled the indicated economic factors in times of high merger activity than in times of low merger activity.

The coincidence of cyclical turning points, alone, cannot be taken as conclusive evidence that capital market conditions are the main immediate cause of increased merger activity. Coincidence in timing may be as much an indication that merger activity responded in the same manner to underlying economic conditions as it is an indication that the capital market is the cause and mergers are the effect. Whatever the causal connection, it seems that the more significant developments are those associated with merger peaks. As the greater dispersion of lags and leads at troughs suggests, the influence of external economic changes in periods of low merger activity is apt to be diffuse and erratic. Their influence in periods of high merger activity, by contrast, is more consistent. Accordingly the greater coincidence of merger peaks with those of the capital market encourages us to look more closely into the behavior of the capital market for clues to the causes of merger revivals.

Correlation with Stock Prices and Industrial Production

Ideally, in bringing correlation analysis to bear, one would examine a variety of factors, each in detail and depth. Practically, it was necessary to restrict the number of analyses, and we shall focus on stock prices and industrial production—series suggested by previous tests as representative of two major types of merger-related forces.

The stock price series was chosen, in preference to the series on the volume of stock trading, as a more direct indicator of the condition of the capital market. The movement of stock prices would seem to be the less equivocal indicator of changes in investor psychology, although both series exhibit high conformity to the reference cycle (see Table 56). For example, it is possible to give a more meaningful interpretation to a rising stock price index in a period of constant trading activity than to a rising volume of trading activity in a period of level stock prices.

116

The index of industrial production was selected as an appropriate indicator of changes in the real level of industrial activity. Short-run changes in the physical volume of output reflect changes in employment and to some degree changes in the applications of technology. The physical volume of industrial production also directly affects the sectors of the economy to which the merger series relate, whereas more comprehensive measures of real economic activity (e.g., deflated gross national product) would be less directly applicable.

Quarterly series of stock prices and of industrial production were computed from available monthly series (Chart 5); they are presented in Table C-7 with a brief description of the method of computation. Their quarterly changes form the basis of correlation analyses for the period 1895-1954.

The stock prices and industrial production series exhibit strong and consistent upward secular trends over the sixty-year period. To avoid "swamping" cyclical movements by trend the two series were adjusted to remove the trend component. The remaining cyclical component was taken as the ratio of the actual value to the trend value for the given quarter. Exponential trends were fitted by use of the least squares method. The underlying straight line shape of the two series, as plotted on semi-logarithmic graphs, indicated this to be a satisfactory form.

The merger series exhibited no clear trend. Indeed, the discontinuous pattern of merger activity suggests that the concept of a secular trend may be inapplicable to mergers. Mergers more strongly reflected the absence than the presence of continuously strong underlying forces, upon which the trend concept is based. This is especially true for the upper stratum of the merger population which our sample represents. We might expect a secularly growing number of mergers of all sizes combined reflecting the growth of the business population. However, it is not likely that the explosive pattern of our series of large mergers is a faithful reflection of the time pattern of mergers among smaller business firms. Moreover, had we tried to specify a trend, the problem of splicing the 1895-1920 and 1919-1954 series would have been formidable.[7] Accordingly no trend-fitting was attempted. As the measure of the "cyclical" pattern of mergers the ratio of the given quarterly value to the average quarterly value for 1895-1920 (or 1919-1954) was used, in the belief that it would provide a satisfactory series of cyclical variations, permitting comparable correlation analyses through the sixty-year period.

[7] On this see Chapter 2.

The correlations between merger disappearances on the one hand and stock prices and industrial production on the other are presented in Table 60. The correlation for the whole sixty-year period

TABLE 60

Simple and Partial Correlation Coefficients among Merger Activity, Stock Prices, and Industrial Production, Quarterly Series of Cyclical Components, 1895–1920

Period and Length of Period	r_{12}	r_{13}	$r_{12.3}$	$r_{13.2}$	r_{23}
1895–1954 (60 years)	+0.469	+0.084	+0.470	+0.085	+0.019
1895–1904 (10 years)	+0.376	+0.304	+0.287	+0.173	+0.421
1905–1918 (14 years)	+0.399	+0.452	+0.013	+0.263	+0.705
1919–1931 (13 years)	+0.713	+0.305	+0.733	+0.384	+0.050
1932–1942 (11 years)	−0.235	−0.124	−0.230	−0.098	+0.114
1943–1954 (12 years)	+0.342	−0.140	+0.317	+0.037	−0.496

X_1 = Cyclical component of merger disappearances series.
X_2 = Cyclical component of industrial stock price series.
X_3 = Cyclical component of industrial production series.

1895–1954 indicates that merger activity paralleled stock-price changes to a much greater degree than it paralleled changes in industrial production.[8] Indeed, the correlation between mergers

[8] Tests of the significance of the departure of observed correlation coefficients from zero, for the 5 per cent and 1 per cent levels of significance, are here summarized:

	5 per cent level of significance				1 per cent level of significance			
Period	r_{12}	r_{13}	$r_{12.3}$	$r_{13.2}$	r_{12}	r_{13}	$r_{12.3}$	$r_{13.2}$
1895–1954	S	N	S	N	S	N	S	N
1895–1904	S	N	N	N	N	N	N	N
1905–1918	S	S	N	N	S	S	N	N
1919–1931	S	S	S	S	S	N	S	S
1932–1942	N	N	N	N	N	N	N	N
1943–1954	N	N	S	N	N	N	N	N

S = Significant departure from zero.
N = Not a significant departure from zero.

In reviewing the stock price series, Sophie Sakowitz of the National Bureau discovered that the splicing ratio used to lower the level of the pre-1914 series to that of the post-1914 series was incorrect. It should have been 0.756 instead of 0.709, as she explained:

"The ratio Nelson used was based on the overlapping period, January 1915–December 1917. However the figures for November 1916 to December 1917 of the second segment had already been raised to the level of the first segment by a ratio based on the figures for October 1916, only. Unfortunately, October 1916 of the first segment was estimated in such a way as to make it very dubious. Therefore all figures based on the ratio using it are equally dubious. The procedure we should use is to lower the segment 1895–1914 (twelve stocks) by the ratio of the following segment (twenty stocks) by the ratio of the actual overlapping data for the period December 1914 to September 1916. This ratio is 0.756."

The pre-1914 series, as corrected by her, is presented in Table C-7. The trend for stock prices and the correlation measures involving stock-price data were not, however,

and industrial production is low enough to raise doubts about the existence of any short-run relationship at all. In part, the low correlation can be attributed to differences in the timing of turning points demonstrated in Tables 56 and 57, which record in another way the lack of short-run parallelism between mergers and industrial production.

The sixty-year period was divided into five subperiods, each at least a decade long, chosen to compare the pattern of response in periods of consistently high merger activity with that in periods of consistently low activity. In periods of low activity we might expect the factor most closely related to the large waves of mergers to exhibit lower correlation with mergers than in periods of high merger activity. As sharp bursts of activity reduce correlations in high-merger periods, the shift between high- and low-activity periods is best examined by comparison with the correlation of the other merger-related variable.

As Table 59 indicates, mergers were more positively correlated to stock-price changes than to changes in industrial production in the three periods of high merger activity—1895–1904, 1919–1931, and 1943–1954. Conversely, in the two periods of low merger activity, 1905–1918 and 1932–1942, industrial production exhibited a higher positive (or lesser negative) relationship to mergers than stock prices did. This suggests that capital market conditions or their underlying causes were of leading importance in periods of high merger activity, and that their role in times of low merger activity was not important. While industrial production was the more important factor in times of low merger activity, the correlations were so low that no strong cause-and-effect connection is suggested.

Brief descriptions of each of the subperiods follow:

1895–1904

The relatively low correlations between mergers and both stock prices and industrial production derive mainly from the difference

recomputed, since it is doubtful that the findings would be changed appreciably. The increase of less than 7 per cent in the level of the pre-1914 data would have a progressively smaller effect on the trend values for the later part of the period. The effect for the period 1895–1914 would, of course, be small, as both the trend and the data would be altered in approximately the same degree.

The Standard Statistics index of industrial production was used in the correlation measures for the period 1895–1918, where it was spliced to the Federal Reserve Board index. Subsequent investigation revealed that the Babson index of business conditions was a somewhat better measure for this early period; it has been substituted for the above measures in Table C-7 and in the turning point comparisons. Again, recalculation of the correlation measures was avoided in the belief that the effects on the findings would not justify the added time and expense.

between the large bursts of merger activity in 1899 and 1901. The 1899 burst was characterized by the merger of many medium-sized firms, while the 1901 burst was characterized by the merger of fewer and larger firms. If the capitalization rather than the number of firms had been the measure used, the merger series would have paralleled more exactly the twin peaks in the production and stock price series. This would have produced higher correlations.

The stock price–merger correlation is higher than the industrial production–merger correlation principally because of the post-1901 time pattern. Industrial production continued to climb through 1902 and into 1903, while both merger activity and stock prices declined steadily from 1901 to late 1903. This suggests that the large merger wave ended not so much in response to an adverse turn in the underlying level of production as to an adverse turn in the condition of the stock market.

The sharp later stage of the decline in stock prices beginning in early 1903 was popularly known as "the rich man's panic." As the name implies, it represented the end of a bull market that had become over-saturated with high-priced securities held largely by a relatively few large investors and speculators. It reflected no serious business depression comparable to that of 1907–1908. The huge merger wave, it is true, exhausted merging opportunities in a number of important industries, and was slowing partly on that account. At any rate, it seems likely that the collapse of the stock market effectively foreclosed remaining merger opportunities, whether many or few.

1905–1918

This period was one of generally low merger activity, and of closely parallel movements in stock prices and industrial production. Perhaps doubly influenced by the reinforcing effects of the two economic forces, merger activity exhibited a fairly high response to their changes. This is reflected both in the timing comparisons made above, and in the moderate positive correlations presented in Table 61, below. Had the merger series been smoothed rather than used in its unsmoothed form, the correlations would have been higher.

Merger activity diminished the sharp business recession of 1907–1908, in which both industrial production and stock prices underwent steep declines. It revived sharply during the recovery in business conditions that reached its peak in 1910. The merger series also closely followed the downward movements of production and stock prices in 1913 and 1914, and responded with equal sensitivity to the 1914–1918 expansion.

Mergers exhibited no strong immediate response to the major anti-trust Supreme Court decisions of 1911, by which the oil, tobacco, and explosives monopolies were dissolved. The merger-depressing effect of these decisions may have been offset by the expansion of stock prices, stock trading, and industrial production that characterized 1911. That the Court decisions may have exerted some inhibiting effect on merger activity is suggested by the fact that these expansions were part of the only set of cycles in these series between 1899 and 1920 for which there was no corresponding merger cycle. But that the Court decisions did not seriously discourage mergers is suggested by the time pattern of merger activity. The years 1911 and 1912 exhibited no sharp decline in merger activity. Rather the decline was very gradual until the second quarter of 1913, by which time declines in stock prices and industrial production were well advanced. It was not until then that merger activity dropped off sharply.

1919–1931

Merger activity increased along with the post-World War I increase in stock prices and industrial production. It reached a peak in 1920, in the same month as the peak in industrial production, and four months after the peak stock-price month. Following this peak, merger activity experienced a protracted three and one-half year decline. This occurred despite the sharp though short cycle in both stock prices and industrial production that was registered in this period. No satisfactory explanation why mergers did not exhibit a cycle comes to mind. The differences in time pattern between the industrial production and stock prices cycles were so small that comparisons were unconvincing. For what it is worth, the stock price cycle was less sharp than the industrial production cycle, and may have been small enough to have had little effect on mergers.

From 1924 through 1929 stock prices increased greatly while industrial production increased only moderately. The merger series more closely followed stock prices. The cyclical component of stock prices, measured as the ratio of the actual value of the series to the trend, rose from a value of 0.90 in mid-1924 to 2.90 in mid-1929, an increase of 193 per cent. In the same period the "cyclical" component of merger disappearances rose from 0.87 to 4.10, an increase of 370 per cent. The cyclical component of industrial production rose from 0.94 to 1.26, an increase of only 28 per cent.

In these five years, the period of the greatest revival of merger activity since the turn of the century, the correlation between stock prices and mergers was higher than at any time in merger history. The correlation between mergers and industrial production was much lower, the moderate increase in industrial production over these five years exhibiting very little relation to the expansion of merger activity.

Comparison of cycles in the three series also attests the importance of stock prices in the late 1920's merger wave. The National Bureau did not designate a cycle in stock prices between 1923 and 1929; however there was a short, sharp peak in stock prices at the end of 1925. This was accompanied by a peak in merger activity in the second quarter of 1926. The corresponding peak in industrial production was not reached until the third quarter of 1927, and roughly coincided with a trough in merger activity.

Following the stock market crash of 1929, the three series declined in roughly parallel fashion. The industrial production series did not decline as sharply as mergers and stock prices; however, its decline was large and unbroken in the manner of the other two. The time patterns of 1929-1932 probably should be regarded as no more than a part of the large and protracted decline in general business activity that dominated these years.

1932-1942

This eleven-year period was noted for the absence of merger activity. It was not until 1942 that merger activity began to revive in any substantial degree. As the correlation measures indicate (Table 59), the response of mergers to the economic forces studied was very small and, if anything, opposite to its response in the three subperiods from 1895 to 1932. The negative correlations are probably more a matter of statistical error than an indication of a meaningful shift in the causal relationship. In this period of very low merger activity we might expect the random appearance of small bursts of merger activity to dominate the correlation measures. This would make a negative and a positive correlation equally probable.

The period can be divided into two parts, each containing unique movements in stock prices and industrial production. The first, spanning the years 1932-1938, is the period of substantial though incomplete recovery from the deep depression of the early 1930's, followed by the sharp, short recession of 1937-1938. In this period stock prices and industrial production were closely parallel, mirroring the business recovery and recession. Merger activity did not respond to these changes with any degree of sensitivity, thus supporting the hypothesis that a serious depression will produce an ebb in merger activity unresponsive even to marked changes in the specific factors related to it.

The second part of this period spans the years 1938–1942, in which the economy underwent a strong protracted recovery to the full and over-full employment levels of World War II. Stock prices and industrial production took divergent courses, however. Stock prices declined moderately and with fair regularity, while industrial production increased markedly and with great regularity. Merger activity remained constant, at the same low levels of 1932–1938, exhibiting no clear tendency either to rise or fall. It was not until the second quarter of 1942, when the stock price index turned up, that merger activity began the protracted rise to its late-1945 peak. In 1942 business activity had apparently revived sufficiently to enable mergers to respond to the stimulus of rising stock prices. The 1937 revival had evidently not been great enough to do so.

1943–1954

The most recent of the five periods is marked by the restoration of merger activity to a sustained level substantially above that of 1932–1942. In only one year, 1949, did the number of merger disappearances fall below that of the most active year of 1932–1942. The average annual number of disappearances for the period 1932–1942 was 125, while that for 1943–1954 was 289.

It is useful to divide the period 1943–1954 into two parts. The first part, 1943–1946, represents a continuation of the wartime divergence in stock prices and industrial production begun in 1938. In a division of merger history according to whether stock prices and industrial production moved in parallel or divergent patterns, the period 1939–1946 would stand out as the period of greatest divergence. Merger activity remained generally low and unresponsive to both stock prices and industrial production until 1942, during a protracted three and one-half year rise in industrial production and an equally protracted fall in stock prices. The 1942 revival of stock prices brought with it the revival of merger activity, and both series began an expansion, which ended in late 1945 for mergers and in early 1946 for stock prices. From 1943 to 1946 both series ran opposite to the decline in industrial production.

The second part of the period, 1947–1954, exhibited a more normal relationship between stock prices and industrial production. There was sufficient divergence between the two series, however, to permit contrasts in the response of merger activity. From 1946 through 1949 mergers followed the small decline in stock prices, running counter, for thirty-three months, to the 1946–1948 rise in industrial production. Following the 1949 trough mergers mirrored the rise in both stock prices and industrial production until 1953. At that time mergers increased sharply, after the manner of stock prices.

1955–1956

Although no quarterly merger series for 1955 and 1956 were available at the time of writing, rough annual comparisons can be made (Table 61). These comparisons indicate that recent merger

TABLE 61

Annual Number of Merger Disappearances, Stock Price Index, and Industrial Production Index, 1954–1956

	Mergers	Industrial Stock Prices	Industrial Production (1947–1949 = 100)
1954	387	334	125
1955	525	443	139
1956	537	493	143
PERCENTAGE CHANGE			
1954–1955	+36	+32	+11
1955–1956	+2	+11	+3
1954–1956	+39	+47	+14

Merger disappearances for 1954 are from *Report on Corporate Mergers and Acquisitions*, Federal Trade Commission, May 1955. For 1955 and 1956, from FTC press releases dated June 18, 1956 and February 14, 1957.

Industrial stock prices: arithmetic average of Dow Jones monthly index published in *Survey of Current Business*, February 1955, 1956, and 1957.

Industrial production index: from the *Federal Reserve Bulletin*, February 1957.

activity corresponded more closely to changes in stock prices than to changes in industrial production. While crude, this finding is consistent with that of the analysis of the quarterly movements in the sixty-year merger history.

Interpretation

Comparison of cyclical turning points indicated that peaks of merger activity were more nearly simultaneous with peaks in stock prices and stock trading, while they led peaks in the reference cycle and industrial production. Merger troughs, on the other hand,

124

showed greater simultaneity with troughs in reference cycles and industrial production, and lagged the troughs of the capital markets series. The indicated greater correlation of mergers with stock prices in periods of high merger activity and of mergers with industrial production in periods of low merger activity may thus have been caused partly by this shift in time sequence. Other things being equal, the correlation of two series with simultaneous turning points will be greater than that of two series with a consistent lead or lag in turning points.

To reduce the bias from this source the subperiods were selected so that each would encompass an integral number of complete cycles in as many of the series as possible. The five periods into which the sixty-year merger history was divided were each sufficiently long to encompass several peaks and troughs (Table 62).

TABLE 62

Number of Peaks and Troughs in Each of Five Subperiods, for Mergers, Stock Prices, and Industrial Production, 1895–1954

Subperiod	Mergers		Stock Prices		Industrial Production	
	Peaks	Troughs	Peaks	Troughs	Peaks	Troughs
1895–1904	2	3	2	3	2	3
1905–1918	3	3	4	4	4	3
1919–1931	2	1	3	2	4	4
1932–1942	0	1	3	4	1	2
1943–1954	1	1	2	2	2	2

No means are at hand for knowing the precise effect of these systematic shifts in timing on the correlation measures, nor the extent to which the selection of subperiods reached this bias, if at all.

The time sequence and the correlation analyses presented above tend to confirm the hypothesis that merger activity was more responsive to economic forces underlying changes in the capital market than to those underlying changes in the level of production. That hypothesis was further confirmed by a detailed examination of short-run changes in mergers and in the two series analyzed, which indicated that the statistical timing and correlation measures were reasonably accurate indicators of the response of mergers to the two kinds of economic change.

The findings do not conclusively demonstrate, however, that underlying industrial factors were not an ultimate factor in merger behavior. It is possible that merger movements represent a burst

125

of industrial reorganization toward which underlying economic and technological developments have been accumulating a long time. A favorable capital market may, under these circumstances, trigger the massive reorganization. Thus, while the findings of the study may have demonstrated clearly the importance of the capital market as a proximate factor in merger movements, they have not so clearly demonstrated its importance as an ultimate cause.

In certain cases it is probably correct to regard the long-run secular trend in an economic series as independent of its short-run cyclical variation. When the cycles are short and relatively small in amplitude, they may be taken as largely "surface phenomena," having no significant effect on underlying growth factors. However, when the series is marked by the infrequent appearance of large bursts of activity, these "cycles" dominate the time pattern and may make inappropriate the concept of gradual underlying forces of change. As infrequent large bursts of activity are likely to be the effect of the equally infrequent appearance of certain short-lived conditions, the cumulative total of activity may be different from that which would result from the smoothing out of the time patterns.

As has been documented in this study, the time series of mergers was characterized by large bursts of activity separated by lengthy intervals of very low activity. Therefore it cannot be claimed that the cumulative amount of merger activity would have been the same if the merger series had behaved like a more normal cycles-on-trend series; nor can it be determined from our data whether the cumulative amount would have been larger or smaller. What does seem certain is that merger activity would have been a good deal less colorful had it followed a more normal time pattern.

The frenzied construction of industrial empires during the large merger waves and their sometimes painful "shaking-down" in the readjustment periods that have followed may or may not have had important effects on the structure and performance of our industrial system. The task in this chapter has been to describe merger patterns and to suggest possible avenues to follow in exploring these questions. The important and interesting job of providing answers remains to be done.

APPENDIX A

CHART A–I
Annual Series of U.S. and British Consolidations, 1887–1904

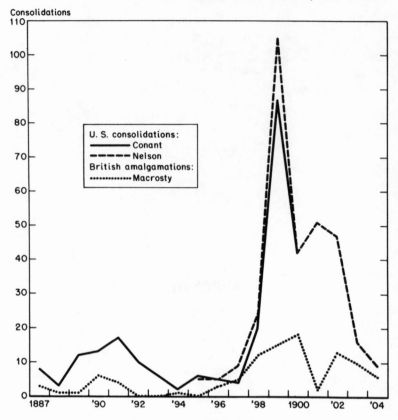

Consolidations

U. S. consolidations:
—————— Conant
— — — — Nelson
British amalgamations:
•••••••••••••••• Macrosty

Appendix A. Comparison of the Early American and British Merger Movements

The United States and Great Britain experienced almost simultaneous early merger waves. In neither country was there evidence of a merger movement of major proportions before the last decade and one-half of the nineteenth century.[1] Both were leading capitalist countries, in which the free market system was the principal organizer of economic activity. This similarity prompts a look at developments in Great Britain as clues to causes of the American merger movement.

The data on the British merger movement are much less detailed, and probably less reliable, than those for the United States. The source used here is *The Trust Movement in British Industry*, by H. W. Macrosty.[2] Macrosty focussed attention on only the more important mergers, and it is uncertain whether these were fully reported. While probably providing a fairly valid picture of the outlines of the movement, the detailed breakdowns by trend and industry are less reliable. However, the study appeared to be sufficiently large for use in making crude tests of merger theories.

The time patterns of mergers in the two countries are presented in Chart A-1. Both Great Britain and the United States experienced bursts of merger activity at the turn of the century, preceded in each case by a smaller flurry of merger activity about ten years earlier. In both countries the consolidation (or amalgamation) was apparently the major form of merger activity throughout this period.

Mergers and Industry Growth Rates

The pattern of industry growth and merger activity in the United States was examined in detail in Chapter 4. It was found that merger movements tended to occur when the growth of the general economy, especially the growth of industries of high merger activity, was characterized by acceleration rather than retardation.

The average annual rates of growth in industrial production by decades for both countries are presented in Table A-1. Five-year moving averages of the two series were computed to smooth the

---

[1] Shannon, in his study of English limited liability companies, indicates no large increase in sales and amalgamations of limited companies until the late 1880's and 1890's. H. A. Shannon, "The Limited Companies of 1866–1883," *Economic History Review*, 1933, reprinted in *Essays in Economic History*, E. M. Carus-Wilson, ed., London, E. Arnold, 1954, p. 384.

[2] London, Longmans, 1907.

TABLE A-1

Annual Perc entage Rates of Growth in Industrial Production, United States and Great
Britain, by Overlapping Decades, 1870–1925

	Average Annual Rate of Growth (per cent)	
Decade	United States	Great Britain
1870–1880	5.8	1.9
1875–1885	6.3	1.4
1880–1890	5.7	2.1
1885–1895	3.8	1.6
1890–1900	3.8	1.7
1895–1905	5.8	2.0
1900–1910	3.8	1.3
1905–1915	3.7	1.3
1910–1920	3.5	−0.9
1915–1925	3.6	−0.5

Based on Indexes of industrial production: for the United States, from W. M. Persons, *Forecasting Business Cycles*, Wiley, 1931, Table 12, pp. 170–171; for Great Britain, from W. G. Hoffman, *British Industry, 1700–1950*, translated by W. O. Henderson and W. H. Chaloner, London, Blackwell, 1955, Table 54, Part B, p. 332.

annual data. The average annual rate of growth for a given decade was obtained by use of the compound interest formula. Throughout the period 1870–1925 British industrial growth was substantially lower than that of the United States. If we were to assume that a merger movement results from an abrupt retardation in high growth rates, as some have claimed for the United States, we would expect the British merger movement to have occurred much earlier in British industrial development than it did, perhaps as early as the 1840's. Since the rate of growth was much lower by 1900, the impact of retardation may have been less; British industry had had time to become adjusted to an economy of low growth rates.

Apart from that qualification, Table A-1 shows that, in both countries, the three overlapping decades 1885–1895, 1890–1900, and 1895–1905 were characterized by increasing rates of industrial growth. It was not until well after the merger movements in both countries that retardation was resumed.

GROWTH RATES OF IMPORTANT MERGER INDUSTRIES

Table A-2 gives a list of important British merger industries compiled from the data presented by Macrosty. Also available are production series relevant to several of these industries,[3] permitting us to examine the growth pattern of specific high-merger industries.

[3] W. G. Hoffman, *British Industry, 1700-1950*, translated by W. O. Henderson and W. H. Chaloner, London, Blackwell, 1955, Table 54, Part B.

TABLE A-2

Industrial Distribution of British Merger Activity, 1887–1906

Industry	Number of Amalgamations	Gross Amalgamation Disappearances
Textiles	34	330
Chemicals	7	156
Mineral extraction	18	138
Iron and steel	29	94
Liquor and beer	14	57
Tobacco	2	16
Other	9	104
	113	895

Source: H. W. Macrosty, *The Trust Movement in British Industry*, London, Longmans, 1907.

The average growth rates of the several series are presented in Table A-3. The picture is mixed. Two of the four industries exhibited sustained acceleration in the period 1885–1905, while two exhibited retardation. If a comprehensive production series had been available for chemicals, one suspects it would have shown acceleration, perhaps tipping the balance in favor of acceleration.

The growth-retardation–merger hypothesis, briefly examined in the light of British experience, seems weak on two counts. First, it fails to explain why Great Britain had a merger movement as late as 1900, when retardation by that time had apparently become

TABLE A-3

Average Annual Decade Rates of Growth, Four British Industries of High Merger Activity, 1870–1925

Decade	Industry			
	Textiles	Iron and Steel	Liquor and Beer	Tobacco
1870–1880	2.1	3.3	1.5	1.5
1875–1885	0.8	3.3	0.1	0.8
1880–1890	1.8	2.8	1.3	1.6
1885–1895	1.4	1.8	2.2	2.3
1890–1900	0.8	2.3	2.2	2.5
1895–1905	0.8	3.2	0.1	2.7
1900–1910	4.8	1.6	−1.4	2.2
1905–1915	2.2	1.7	−0.8	2.0
1910–1920	−1.1	−1.2	−3.0	0.4
1915–1925	−3.4	−2.3	−2.8	2.7
Number of series	4	2	3	1

Source: Hoffman, *British Industry, 1700–1950*, Table 54, Part B.

a long-established pattern. Second, the balance of evidence is slightly in favor of the thesis that mergers were a more common feature of industries undergoing growth acceleration.

TRANSPORTATION DEVELOPMENT AND MERGERS

The patterns of transportation growth in England and the United States were quite different. By 1900 the British railway net had been long achieved, while that of the United States was just reaching full development.[4] This is reflected in differences in the rates of growth of railroad freight haulage in the two countries (Table A-4). In addition, the geographical concentration of British

TABLE A-4

Annual Percentage Rates of Growth, Railroad Freight Haulage,
United States and Great Britain, 1885–1910

Decade	United States[a]	Great Britain[b]
1885–1895	6.0	2.6
1890–1900	6.0	3.2
1895–1905	8.2	3.5
1900–1910	6.4	2.1

[a] Based on ton-miles data.
[b] Based on tons of freight hauled.

Source: for the United States, *Historical Statistics of the United States, 1789–1945*, Bureau of the Census, 1949; for Great Britain, Hoffman, *British Industry, 1700–1950*, Table 54, Part B.

industry was necessarily much higher than that of the United States. The area east of the Mississippi River alone was almost ten times that of Great Britain. It therefore seems unlikely that the low rate of British railroad growth in the late nineteenth century was responsible for the destruction of isolated local monopolies with a consequent increase in the need to merge. Such a force, if operating, probably would have been greatest at a much earlier date.

Developments in the tariff, a factor in the effect of international transportation changes on the competitive positions of industries, seem to have taken divergent courses in the two countries. British industry, which had operated under a policy of free trade for decades, continued to do so through the period of high merger activity. United States industry, on the other hand, had long been

[4] The development of the pre-railroad network of canals in Great Britain also preceded that of the United States. The Manchester–Liverpool canal was completed in 1772; the Erie Canal, in 1825.

operating under a policy of protection, enhanced in the late 1900's by a series of almost uninterrupted tariff increase from 1883 to 1897.[5] It was not until the Underwood Act of 1913 that a reduction in tariffs was enacted. The American argument that "the tariff was the mother of the trusts" thus receives little support from the British experience.

Mergers and the Capital Market

The relationship between the capital market and the early merger wave in the United States was examined in detail in Chapter 4. The evidence suggested that the capital market played a central role in the merger movement. The organized securities exchanges underwent important quantitative and qualitative growth in the years preceding and during the merger movement. Many consolidations used the organized exchanges to market their securities, and merger activity responded more sensitively to changes in stock prices than to changes in industrial production.

No series could be found on the volume of trading on the organized British securities exchanges, or on other magnitudes relating to their ability to handle the large securities issues accompanying the wave of amalgamations at the end of the century. However, there are several historical reasons for believing that the British capital market had attained maturity before that of the United States. Among them is the head start in general industrial growth enjoyed by Great Britain, with the necessary development of financial institutions for gathering and allocating capital. The export of large amounts of capital to the United States in the middle and late nineteenth century further reflected the existence of an organized system for marshalling capital. Finally, as the financial center for a vast nineteenth-century colonial empire, the British Isles probably nurtured the growth of financial institutions beyond what was needed for strictly domestic purposes. We may say with reasonable assurance that the capital market, by the end of the nineteenth century, was adequate to support a large merger wave.

The early development of the British capital market tends to rule it out as an immediate cause of the merger movement. In this respect the British experience differs from that of the United States. However, a limited examination of the relationship between mergers and stock prices indicates that British merger activity responded in a positive fashion to capital market conditions. Table

[5] See F. W. Taussig, *The Tariff History of the United States*, Putnam, 1931.

A-5 gives the results of correlating the number of firms disappearing annually into amalgamations with the securities quotation index and the industrial production index for the nineteen-year period of high British merger activity, 1886–1904.

TABLE A-5

Relationship of Merger Activity to Stock Prices and Industrial Production, Great Britain, 1886–1904, United States, 1895–1904

	Great Britain (annually)	United States (quarterly)
Coefficients of simple correlation between—		
Mergers and securities prices	+0.550	+0.613
Mergers and industrial production	+0.530	+0.259
Securities prices and industrial production	+0.939	+0.659
Coefficients of partial correlation between—		
Mergers and securities prices, after allowing for changes in industrial production	+0.178	+0.608
Mergers and industrial production, after allowing for changes in stock prices	+0.049	−0.243

Source: Annual series on merger disappearances in Great Britain, Macrosty, *The Trust Movement in British Industry*; on security quotations and industrial production index, Hoffman, *British Industry, 1700–1950*. The coefficients for the United States are based on quarterly series in Tables B-1, B-2, and C-7, below.

The correlation coefficients indicate that British merger activity was slightly more responsive to changes in stock prices than to changes in industrial production. But, since the correlation between stock prices and industrial production is very high, the separate effect of these two variables cannot be demonstrated as clearly for Great Britain as it was for the United States. In any case, the British experience seems to have been similar in general outline to that of the United States, and the findings tend to support the hypothesis that the capital market played an important role in the early merger movement in this country. This supplementary evidence based upon a necessarily crude analysis can only be fortified by more detailed examinations of the British experience, yet to be made.

Judicial Interpretation of Antitrust Legislation

A frequent explanation of the early merger wave in the United States is that combination by merger was the only legal way to control competition. Two leading Supreme Court decisions are usually cited to show that the Courts interpreted the section of the Sherman Act[6] prohibiting the monopolization of an industry (section 2) very narrowly, while they interpreted the section prohibiting conspiracies in restraint of trade (section 1) very broadly. The narrow interpretation of section 2 was made in 1895 in the Knight decision, five years after the passage of the Sherman Act.[7] The broader interpretation of section 1 came in 1899 in the Addyston Pipe decision.[8] It is argued that these decisions informed businessmen that looseknit associations—pools and cartels—would receive harsh Court treatment, and that mergers would receive lenient Court treatment.

The timing of the Court decisions does not fit this hypothesis very well. The anticonspiracy Addyston decision was not made until 1899, after many consolidations had been consummated. However, the Circuit Court decision of William Howard Taft, which may have been regarded as definitive even though appealed to the Supreme Court, was made on February 8, 1898.[9] Two other anticonspiracy decisions that may have been regarded as setting the precedent also occurred in the initial stages of the large merger wave.[10] The picture is therefore mixed. Certainly the timing of Court decisions is not clear enough to permit a simple cause-and-effect explanation of the switch from pools and cartels to mergers as the leading device for securing market control. It also fails to explain the brief flurry of mergers in 1888–1892.

The leading English antitrust decision of this period was the Mogul decision of December 1891.[11] England had no statutory provisions for dealing with the monopoly problem. The decision was an interpretation of the English common law regarding conspiracies in restraint of trade. The Mogul Steamship Company sued a combination of shipping companies for damages to Mogul by rebates offered shippers confining their shipments of Hankow tea exclusively to the conspiring companies. Judgement was given unanimously against the Mogul Company. In effect, the decision made such conspiracies in restraint more permissible rather than less.

Opinion differs as to the degree to which the Mogul decision represented a departure from the English common law tradition

[6] An Act to Protect Trade and Commerce Against Unlawful Restraints and Monopolies, July 2, 1890, 26 Stat. L. 209.
[7] United States v. E. C. Knight Co., 156 U.S. 1 (1895).
[8] Addyston Pipe and Steel Co. v. United States, 175 U.S. 211 (1899).
[9] Addyston Pipe and Steel Co. v. United States, 271, *Federal Reporter*, April–May 1898.
[10] United States v. Trans-Missouri Freight Association, 166 U.S. 290 (1897), and United States v. Joint Traffic Association, 171 U.S. 505 (1898).
[11] Mogul Steamship Co. v. McGregor, Dow and Co., 1892, A.C. 25.

of hostility toward such conspiracies. One view is that it represented a sharp break with the tradition.[12] Another view is that it was only one, though an important one, of a series of decisions that had been progressively modifying that hostility.[13] Whether a sharp or gradual break from tradition, the interpretation of the English courts ran counter to the anti-conspiracy decisions of the American Courts. This lends scant support to the hypothesis that, in the United States, judicial interpretation shaped the pattern of industrial combination.

Corporation Law Changes

The liberalization of the corporation laws of certain states in the late 1880's and 1890's has been offered as one of the proximate causes of the United States merger movement.[14] These changes included more lenient provisions for obtaining charters from corporation commissions, lifting of narrow restrictions on lines of business permitted, raising limits on authorized capitalization, and permission for a corporation to own the stock of another corporation. Without this permissive legislation, it is argued, a widespread merger movement would have been prevented.

The major development in English law bearing on the freedom and size of corporations was the granting of general limited liability to ordinary trading and manufacturing companies by act of Parliament. In addition to introducing a general limited liability, the acts did away with many of the regulatory provisions that had characterized earlier corporation laws.[15] It was an abrupt change in English law comparable to the later liberalizations in American law achieved when New Jersey and Delaware began the competition for incorporating business enterprises.

The English Limited Liability Act was passed in 1855, and repealed and further liberalized in the Joint Stock Companies Act of 1856. These laws were followed almost immediately by a large increase in the number of incorporations. Between 1844 and 1855,

[12] F. H. Levy, "A Contrast Between the Antitrust Laws of Foreign Countries and of the United States," *Annals of the American Academy of Political and Social Science*, January 1930, p. 128.

[13] Hans B. Thorelli, *The Federal Antitrust Policy, Origination of An American Tradition*, Johns Hopkins Press, 1955, pp. 27–35.

[14] George J. Stigler, "Monopoly and Oligopoly by Merger" *Papers and Proceedings of the American Economic Association*, May 1950, pp. 27–31.

[15] H. A. Shannon, "The Coming of General Limited Liability," *Economic History Review*, 1931, reprinted in *Essays in Economic History*, *op. cit.*, p. 378.

966 unlimited liability companies registered under the Registration Act of 1844. The total number of limited liability companies registered between 1856 and 1862 was 2479.[16] Table A-6 shows an unbroken increase in incorporations from the 1860's into the 1930's (where the data ends).

TABLE A-6

Number of Business Incorporations in the United Kingdom
by Nine-Year Periods, 1856–1937

Period	Number of Incorporations	
	Shannon	Evans
1856–1865	4,859	
1866–1874	6,111	6,660
1875–1883	9,551	10,570
1884–1892		19,785
1893–1901		37,172
1902–1910		44,069
1911–1919		53,348
1920–1928		76,575
1929–1937		103,707

Source: Shannon, "The Limited Companies of 1866–1883," p. 382; George H. Evans, Jr., *Business Incorporations in the United States, 1800–1943*, National Bureau of Economic Research, 1948, Table 14, p. 35.

The forty-odd year lag between the limited liability acts of 1855–1856 and the turn-of-the-century merger movement disqualifies the acts as immediate causes of the merger wave. During this period, moreover, there were no further major liberalizations of the law that would drastically ease the regulation of corporations. The law was made sufficiently liberal in its first enactment.

There were, however, important qualitative changes in the use of limited liability charters in the years from 1856 until shortly before the merger wave. In the years immediately following the 1855–1856 acts, high par-value shares were commonly issued, partially paid-up, and with promises not to call for the remainder of the subscription. Arrangements like these, commonly with only a few investors, amounted largely to a continuation of the unlimited liability partnership organization which had traditionally characterized English business. In the 1880's, the more common form of limited liability share arrangement was low par value, fully paid up, and many investors. As in the modern large corporation, the investors' liability was truly limited to the amount of the

[16] *Ibid.*, p. 379.

original investment, and ownership was more fully divorced from control.[17]

The British corporate law experience, as a guide to causes of the United States merger movement, presents a mixed picture. The necessary legislative changes took place some forty years before the merger wave; but apparently it took nearly that long to change the manner of business operation and financing to realize fully the potentialities of limited liability. Business in the United States had also operated under limited liability laws for an extended period, so that by tradition and experience it was prepared to exploit the liberalized features of the acts of the 1880's and 1890's. These features, in effect, had existed in British law since 1856. If, as is likely, the unlimited liability partnership tradition was not as strong in the United States as in Britain, it seems probable that the United States would have experienced an earlier rise in merger activity if corporation laws had been made more lenient at an earlier date. This is largely conjectural, however, and must await more definitive studies for a final answer.

[17] This paragraph draws almost exclusively upon J. B. Jeffreys' article, "The Denomination and Character of Shares, 1855–1885," *Economic History Review*, 1946, reprinted in *Essays in Economic History, op. cit.*, pp. 344–357.

Appendix B. Basic Tables on Merger Activity

Total Merger Capitalizations, Quarterly, 1895–1920[a]

(thousands of dollars)

Year and Quarter		Manufacturing	Mining	Total Manufacturing and Mining
1895	1	984		984
	2	10,352		20,352
	3	14,500		14,500
	4	458		458
1896	1	6,050		6,050
	2	4,500		4,500
	3			
	4	1,265		1,265
1897	1	10,000		10,000
	2			
	3	81,600		81,600
	4	10,275	1,025	11,300
1898	1	167,542		167,542
	2	44,736		47,736
	3	209,306		209,306
	4	212,324		212,324
1899	1	862,580	9,750	952,330
	2	522,432	8,780	531,212
	3	373,404	67,000	440,404
	4	112,874	30,000	146,414
1900	1	149,943	2,500	157,755
	2	126,900	6,350	133,250
	3	98,300	5,000	103,300
	4	11,800	1,100	16,884
1901	1	139,457		139,457
	2	1,601,728	32,000	1,636,383
	3	94,898	8,488	103,386
	4	87,233	33,220	121,853
1902	1	205,814	54,000	259,814
	2	135,352	95,858	252,095
	3	258,066	1,500	259,566
	4	84,998	2,250	87,248
1903	1	84,446	21,544	105,990
	2	22,056	31,000	53,056
	3	30,989	6,349	38,666
	4	24,490	38,703	63,193
1904	1	28,807	250	29,057
	2	15,500	8,744	24,244
	3	4,100		4,100
	4	9,887	9,944	19,831
1905	1	46,286	11,000	57,286
	2	37,985	44,957	83,942
	3	30,903	15,700	46,603
	4	20,416	8,614	29,030

TABLE B-1, continued

Year and Quarter		Manufacturing	Mining	Total Manufacturing and Mining
1906	1	114,229	23,500	139,499
	2	21,285	50,750	80,003
	3	18,168		21,168
	4	18,010	67,210	85,220
1907	1	18,057	31,744	49,801
	2	37,199	5,764	42,963
	3	34,532	3,605	38,137
	4	35,487	2,744	38 231
1908	1	6 250	13,400	19,650
	2	18,817	10,000	28,817
	3	61,000		61,000
	4	38,505	25,000	63,505
1909	1	8,340	650	8,990
	2	26,600	6,244	32,844
	3	11,276	8,850	20,126
	4	17,508	2,000	19,508
1910	1	37,710	20,200	65,910
	2	51,070	48,524	99,594
	3	44,148		45,476
	4	18,869	5,542	24,411
1911	1	34,921	1,000	35,921
	2	56,381	8,900	65,281
	3	5,834	1,100	21,934
	4	39,145	33,580	76,725
1912	1	71,214		72,099
	2	82,712		82,712
	3	64,928		64,928
	4	82,121	8,232	90,353
1913	1	65,803	3,250	80,053
	2	18,691	8,000	37,691
	3	17,000		17,885
	4	17,455	95	17,550
1914	1	39,634		39,634
	2	74,492		74,492
	3	5,578		5,578
	4	32,930		32,930
1915	1	3,563	425	3,988
	2	49,141		49,141
	3	14,835		14,835
	4	71,167	1,421	78,588
1916	1	106,199		106,199
	2	147,895	8,532	156,427
	3	59,500		61,500
	4	110,724	1,626	112,350
1917	1	140,541	502	141,143
	2	85,947	9,280	95,227
	3	68,283	34,030	102,313
	4	291,409	5,975	297,384

TABLE B-1, concluded

Year and Quarter		Manufacturing	Mining	Total Manufacturing and Mining
1918	1	26,670	11,620	38,290
	2	55,632	42,320	97,952
	3	41,095		41,095
	4	26,151	8,000	34,151
1919	1	56,944	7,040	66,734
	2	372,296	95,020	467,316
	3	177,444	12,460	189,904
	4	185,117	14,051	199,268
1920	1	207,320	31,218	241,488
	2	160,118	21,279	181,397
	3	179,456	9,800	189,256
	4	387,757	14,620	402,377

a For industries included, see Table B-3. "Total manufacturing and mining" includes the two mixed groups not assignable to either manufacturing or mining. Quarterly figures sum to less than annual totals (Table B-3) because of a small number of cases in which sufficiently exact dates were not available.

TABLE B-2

Disappearances by Consolidation (C) and by Acquisition (A), Quarterly, 1895–1920[a]

Year and Quarter		Manufacturing		Mining		Total Manufacturing and Mining	
		C[b]	A	C[b]	A	C[b]	A
1895	1		3				3
	2	4	1			13	1
	3	24				24	
	4		1				1
1896	1	2	1			2	1
	2	7				7	
	3						
	4		1				1
1897	1	8				8	
	2						
	3	38				38	
	4	14	2		1	14	3
1898	1	131	1			131	1
	2	34	3			61	3
	3	17	2			17	2
	4	70	4			70	4

141

TABLE B-2, continued

Year and Quarter	Manufacturing		Mining		Total Manufacturing and Mining	
	C^b	A	C^b	A	C^b	A
1899 1	384	8	4		402	8
2	252	9	9	1	261	10
3	189	17	110		299	17
4	32	5	87		119	9
1900 1	125	6	12		137	10
2	41	4	9	1	50	5
3	57	2	1		58	2
4	44	3	2	1	46	7
1901 1	86	11			86	11
2	62	11	30	4	102	18
3	44	7	8	2	52	9
4	33	8	62	5	99	13
1902 1	40	17	53	3	93	20
2	24	20	5	3	33	24
3	84	11		1	84	12
4	48	16	3		51	16
1903 1	33	7		5	33	12
2	6	11	4	1	10	12
3	9	22		3	9	26
4	2	7	2	3	4	10
1904 1	14	12		1	14	13
2	13			2	13	2
3		4				4
4	3	6	6	2	9	8
1905 1	33	12	9	1	42	13
2	16	9	20	14	38	23
3	2	11	45	2	47	13
4	5	6	11	1	16	7
1906 1	4	10	5	1	9	13
2	4	6	22	3	26	15
3		10			3	10
4		12	8	2	8	14
1907 1	9	10	13	12	22	22
2	14	3		3	14	6
3	13	2		1	13	3
4		4		1		5
1908 1	1	1	2	1	3	2
2	2	5	2		4	5
3	10	1			10	1
4	9	4	3		12	4
1909 1	1	2		1	1	3
2	8	2		3	8	5
3		4	1	1	1	5
4	1	14	1		2	14
1910 1	21	15	11	1	46	16
2	5	16	9	6	14	22
3	15	6			15	7
4		12		2		14

TABLE B-2, concluded

Year and Quarter	Manufacturing C^b	Manufacturing A	Mining C^b	Mining A	Total Manufacturing and Mining C^b	Total Manufacturing and Mining A
1911 1	4	4		1	4	5
2	31	6	9	1	40	7
3		5		1	8	6
4	4	5	1	2	17	7
1912 1	8	11			8	12
2	21	10			21	10
3	7	5			7	5
4	1	9		3	1	12
1913 1	6	17	4		11	17
2		8	3		20	8
3	3	1			3	2
4	2	4		1	2	5
1914 1	12	8			12	8
2		3				3
3	1	4			1	4
4	6	1			6	1
1915 1		3		1		4
2	10	12			10	12
3	2	6			2	6
4	10	13		1	14	14
1916 1	3	10			3	10
2	21	19		6	21	25
3	5	8			8	8
4	13	18		1	13	19
1917 1	22	30		2	22	33
2	13	12	7	4	20	16
3	4	23	11	8	15	31
4	24	11	2		26	11
1918 1		16		3		19
2	4	9	1	3	5	12
3		14				14
4		10		1		11
1919 1	4	10		3	4	15
2	27	8	6	9	33	17
3	27	24	2	3	29	27
4	10	21	4	2	14	24
1920 1	13	44	5	10	18	56
2	5	38		5	5	43
3	5	21		2	5	23
4	19	19		4	19	23

[a] For industries included, see Table B-3. "Total manufacturing and mining" includes the two mixed groups not assignable to either manufacturing or mining. Quarterly figures sum to less than annual totals (Table B-7) because of a small number of cases in which sufficiently exact dates were not available.

[b] The figure for consolidation disappearance is net, e.g., when one company is formed by the union of six companies, the net number of firm disappearances is five.

Year	Ordnance	Food	Tobacco	Textiles	Apparel	Lumber	Furniture	Pap
1895			1,794					
1896		2,315						
1897		79,286	60				6,000	
1898		103,896	99,723	12,000				50,0
1899		304,463	82,377	113,030		6,000	10,000	60,3
1900		60,564	26,661	5,000				3,6
1901		54,108	28,934	60,641		10,000		9
1902	10,000	128,436	49,792			10,908		36,3
1903		21,464	17,842	1,648	1,048			3,2
1904		22,758	416					1,0
1905		44,558	2,469	1,092			3,000	
1906		103,575	5,821	7,750	1,000	3,500		1,7
1907		29,249		15,000		5,000		2,6
1908		7,217		19,000				1,0
1909		6,406		8,480				
1910		10,800	8,000	22,323			1,977	
1911		23,550		13,554				
1912		30,925	51,168	4,895	8,000	15,816		
1913		1,052	8,768	4,911				
1914		19,097		15,234				3,9
1915	11,162	6,275	1,708	11,300			3,221	
1916	5,904	34,347	1,708	13,900	1,000	3,221		3,3
1917	19,080	25,857	2,823	5,770				5,7
1918	5,554	7,228	1,854	200				3,5
1919	3,054	69,056	15,933	56,700				2,3
1920	3,054	34,609	5,074	10,829	1,000		2,000	12,6
1895–1904	10,000	777,290	307,599	192,319	1,048	26,908	16,000	155,5
1905–1914		276,429	76,226	112,239	9,000	24,316	4,977	8,8
1915–1920	47,808	177,372	29,098	98,699	2,000	3,221	5,221	27,7
1895–1920	57,808	1,231,091	412,923	403,257	12,048	54,445	26,198	192,2

TABLE

Year	Machineryb	Electrical Machinery	Transportation Equipment	Instruments	Miscellaneous Manufacturing	Total Manufacturing	Metal Minin
1895		7,000				30,770	
1896		12,500			3,500	24,691	
1897	4,000		6,000			115,021	4,630
1898	12,567	2,500		880	20,000	647,569	
1899	75,850	10,000	287,031	11,800	13,862	2,063,625	18,530
1900	19,035	18,000	28,420	1,000		417,073	5,000
1901	71,010	22,000	50,000	3,500	1,350	1,963,061	21,500
1902	151,644	2,600	2,911	950	18,931	725,295	88,614
1903	33,420	1,880	718	4,800	11,977	190,071	42,210
1904	3,458	1,880	1,018		1,977	91,545	
1905	27,034		6,083			160,397	7,219
1906	10,916	2,301				205,380	127,973
1907	13,858		300		4,954	135,588	32,463
1908		22,750	60,700		12,000	139,160	25,000
1909	2,180		11,432	1,500		71,397	2,500
1910	26,985		38,678			173,466	
1911	21,948		10,000		12,454	144,028	31,100
1912	58,380	3,760	17,052	11,000	1,977	313,290	
1913	8,154		4,813			135,319	8,095
1914				880		156,030	3,614
1915	16,226	4,389	38,059			152,536	1,846
1916	10,326	1,553	134,729	6,442		456,981	85
1917	15,152		35,631		669	628,400	3,480
1918	15,500	2,770	62,571			187,227	14,000
1919	7,677	5,500	61,615		446	853,863	85
1920	33,537	20,022	82,993	3,221	223	983,826	1,775
1895–1904	370,984	78,360	376,098	22,930	71,597	6,268,721	180,484
1905–1914	169,455	28,811	149,058	13,380	31,385	1,634,055	237,96
1915–1920	98,418	34,234	415,598	9,663	1,338	3,262,833	22,80
1895–1920	638,857	141,405	940,757	45,973	104,320	11,165,609	441,24

b Except electrical.

g	Chemicals	Petroleum, Coal	Rubber	Leather	Stone, Glass	Primary Metals	Metal Products a	Year
	6,500	1,000			10,000	4,476		1895
	376	5,000					1,000	1896
			675			19,000		1897
	43,575	11,100				289,528	1,800	1898
	154,985	30,000	58,401	35,000	50,500	698,012	62,000	1899
	2,028	22,000		1,000	27,365	117,650	78,700	1900
	42,479		10,000		14,000	1,496,199	97,908	1901
	11,199				28,985	227,932	40,647	1902
	28,238	15,000		3,500	1,355	43,631	300	1903
	3,564				3,000	46,618	3,829	1904
	1,912		5,401	4,531	10,000	34,074	13,243	1905
	4,233		7,250			56,972		1906
	3,000	955		1,015	710	55,926	3,461	1907
	5,688					8,976	1,829	1908
	24,000		4,000		123	12,276		1909
	5,495	5,739			1,240	42,101	10,128	1910
	6,084			21,000		21,359	8,829	1911
		8,743		22,413	3,600		75,361	1912
	7,740	39,156	10,802	1,015		25,579	23,329	1913
	13,288	20,000	5,401		300	75,092	829	1914
	19,285	6,339	1,430			31,229	1,913	1915
	15,741	101,629	2,710		7,500	107,980	4,916	1916
	292,475	99,302	18,370		150	75,976	23,865	1917
	20,607	7,945	1,430		3,750	38,858	15,396	1918
	4,750	445,045	1,430	4,000	11,150	125,668	36,229	1919
	306,516	239,678	1,430	6,442	40,465	125,049	55,006	1920
	292,944	73,000	80,176	39,500	135,205	2,943,046	286,184	1895–1904
	80,183	65,850	55,537	31,161	12,373	407,716	61,848	1905–1914
	659,374	899,938	26,800	10,442	63,015	504,760	137,325	1915–1920
	1,032,501	1,038,788	162,513	81,013	210,593	3,852,122	485,357	1895–1920

ept ordnance, machinery, and transportation equipment.

ued

inous al	Petroleum and Gas Extraction	Nonmetal Minerals c	Total Mining	Ice	Nonallocable	Total Manufacturing and Mining	Year
				10,000		40,770	1895
						24,691	1896
630			4,630	3,000		119,651	1897
		3,000	115,530	60,000	23,540	650,569	1898
000	100	9,500	14,950	9,296	885	2,262,695	1899
350		12,100	86,808	1,400	2,655	442,204	1900
208	40,000	1,500	161,352		24,160	2,053,924	1901
238	303		106,201	1,328		910,807	1902
688		250	18,988			297,600	1903
738						110,533	1904
302	3,100	3,150	80,271	2,328		242,996	1905
700	1,000	10,000	159,673	7,968	4,770	377,791	1906
744		2,650	43,857	5,312		184,757	1907
		23,400	48,400			187,560	1908
594		3,650	17,744			89,141	1909
064	14,060	1,142	74,266	9,328		257,060	1910
244	5,736		44,080	6,328	15,000	209,436	1911
232			8,232		885	322,407	1912
488		3,250	16,833	22,000	885	175,037	1913
			3,614			159,644	1914
			1,846	6,000		160,382	1915
980	552	1,626	11,008	2,000		469,989	1916
375	20,780	77	50,212		100	678,712	1917
480	5,460	8,000	61,940	5,000		254,167	1918
380	60,140	12,626	128,996	2,650	200	985,709	1919
584	59,278		103,737	2,950		1,090,513	1920
222	40,403	26,350	508,459	85,024	51,240	6,913,444	1895–1904
368	23,896	47,242	496,970	53,264	21,540	2,205,829	1905–1914
899	146,210	22,329	357,739	18,600	300	3,639,472	1915–1920
489	210,509	95,921	1,363,168	156,888	73,080	12,758,745	1895–1920

pt fuels.

Year	Ordnance	Food	Tobacco	Textiles	Apparel	Lumber	Furniture	Pap
1895								
1896								
1897		75,600					6,000	
1898		100,600	95,000	12,000				50,0
1899		294,400	20,000	113,030		6,000	10,000	58,0
1900		54,000	25,000	5,000				3,1
1901		34,000	20,000	60,000		10,000		
1902	10,000	107,750	13,500			3,000		35,5
1903		3,000	12,000					3,2
1904		12,000						
1905		20,500					3,000	
1906		80,000		7,000	1,000			
1907		24,000		14,500		5,000		
1908		3,000		19,000				
1909								
1910		10,000	8,000	20,000				
1911		20,000		10,000				
1912		30,000	50,000	1,103	8,000			
1913				1,680				
1914		12,000		13,550				3,0
1915	2,000	5,000		10,500				
1916		29,028		13,000				
1917				2,500				2,0
1918		2,073						
1919		59,416	11,215	53,820				
1920		10,990	4,220					3,9
1895–1904	10,000	681,350	185,500	190,030		19,000	16,000	149,9
1905–1914		199,500	58,000	86,833	9,000	5,000	3,000	3,0
1915–1920	2,000	106,507	15,435	79,820				5,9
1895–1920	12,000	987,357	258,935	356,683	9,000	24,000	19,000	158,

Year	Machineryb	Electrical Machinery	Transportation Equipment	Instruments	Miscellaneous Manufacturing	Total Manufacturing	Meta Mini
1895		7,000				24,500	
1896		12,500			3,500	22,000	
1897	4,000		6,000			110,600	
1898	11,000				20,000	612,400	
1899	75,850	10,000	282,300	11,800	1,000	1,893,180	14,75
1900	13,450	16,000	18,000	1,000		374,850	5,00
1901	68,500	22,000	50,000	3,500	1,350	1,833,650	19,00
1902	128,000				13,000	540,400	85,00
1903	28,500				10,000	111,250	30,00
1904						26,000	
1905	10,000		1,500			64,375	
1906						103,000	82,55
1907	12,500				1,000	66,125	
1908		22,750	60,000		12,000	120,750	25,00
1909	1,500		1,000			26,500	
1910			10,000			58,050	
1911	18,000		10,000		8,500	102,750	30,00
1912	54,000		1,000	11,000		188,603	
1913						32,380	8,00
1914						61,050	
1915	2,000		33,750			68,325	
1916	5,000		114,314			205,977	
1917	4,500		5,928			375,141	2,0
1918	15,500		20,000			40,173	14,0
1919	2,351	2,000	15,409			551,922	
1920	10,484	10,689	39,296			524,510	
1895–1904	329,350	67,500	356,300	16,300	48,850	5,548,830	153,7
1905–1914	96,500	22,750	83,500	11,000	21,500	823,583	145,5
1915–1920	39,835	12,689	228,699			1,766,048	16,0
1895–1920	465,685	102,939	668,497	27,300	70,350	8,138,461	315,

b Except electrical

Chemicals	Petroleum, Coal	Rubber	Leather	Stone, Glass	Primary Metals	Metal Products[a]	Year
6,500	1,000			10,000			1895
	5,000					1,000	1896
					19,000		1897
43,500		2,500			276,000	1,800	1898
118,000	30,000	53,000	35,000	50,500	662,300	62,000	1899
	22,000			26,300	106,250	78,700	1900
38,300		10,000		13,500	1,408,500	94,000	1901
4,000				27,600	160,000	34,000	1902
25,000	15,000		3,500	1,000	10,000		1903
3,000				3,000	5,000	3,000	1904
				10,000	1,500	10,875	1905
					15,000		1906
					8,025	1,100	1907
4,000							1908
24,000							1909
2,050						8,000	1910
1,000			21,000		1,000	8,000	1911
4,000					29,000		1912
6,000	2,200					22,500	1913
12,500	20,000						1914
	5,000				10,075		1915
10,000	17,500				17,135		1916
267,853	47,000	15,360			6,500	16,000	1917
						2,600	1918
2,500	318,893		4,000	7,400	49,332	25,586	1919
287,114	41,559			14,215	102,000		1920
238,300	73,000	65,500	38,500	131,900	2,647,050	274,500	1895–1904
53,550	22,200		21,000	10,000	54,525	50,475	1905–1914
567,467	429,952	15,360	4,000	21,615	185,042	44,186	1915–1920
859,317	525,152	80,860	63,500	163,515	2,886,617	369,161	1895–1920

:ept ordnance, machinery, and transportation equipment.

ued

minous oal	Petroleum and Gas Extraction	Nonmetal Minerals[c]	Total Mining	Ice	Nonallocable	Total Manufacturing and Mining	Year
				10,000		34,500	1895
						22,000	1896
						110,600	1897
				3,000		615,400	1898
,000		3,000	111,750	60,000	20,000	2,084,930	1899
		9,500	14,500			389,350	1900
,000		12,100	62,100	1,400		1,897,150	1901
,500	40,000	1,500	144,000		10,000	694,400	1902
000			36,000			147,250	1903
000			5,000			31,000	1904
600		2,500	40,100	1,000		105,475	1905
300		10,000	109,850		3,600	215,850	1906
500			1,500			67,625	1907
		22,750	47,750			168,500	1908
,500		2,000	9,500			36,000	1909
000	14,060		49,060	8,000		115,110	1910
,000	4,900		37,900	5,000	15,000	160,650	1911
						188,603	1912
		3,250	11,250	22,000		65,630	1913
						61,050	1914
				6,000		74,325	1915
				2,000		211,198	1916
,975	10,000		25,975			401,116	1917
			14,000			54,173	1918
,500	44,000	7,000	58,500			610,422	1919
,764	25,000		32,764			557,274	1920
,500	40,000	26,100	373,350	74,400	30,000	6,026,580	1895–1904
,900	18,960	40,500	306,910	36,000	18,000	1,184,493	1905–1914
,239	79,000	7,000	131,239	8,000		1,905,287	1915–1920
,639	137,960	73,600	811,499	118,400	48,000	9,116,360	1895–1920

:ept fuels.

Year	Ordnance	Food	Tobacco	Textiles	Apparel	Lumber	Furniture	
1895			1,794					
1896		2,315						
1897		3,686	60					
1898		3,296	4,723					
1899		10,063	62,377					2
1900		6,564	1,661					
1901		20,108	8,934	641				
1902		20,686	36,292			7,908		
1903		18,464	5,842	1,648	1,048			
1904		10,758	416					
1905		24,058	2,469	1,092				
1906		23,575	5,821	750		3,500		
1907		5,249		500				
1908		4,217						
1909		6,406		8,480				
1910		800		2,323			1,977	
1911		3,550		3,554				
1912		925	1,168	3,792		15,816		
1913		1,052	8,768	3,231				
1914		7,097		1,684				
1915	9,162	1,275	1,708	800			3,221	
1916	5,904	5,319	1,708	900	1,000	3,221		
1917	19,080	25,857	2,823	3,270				
1918	5,554	5,155	1,854	200				
1919	3,054	9,640	4,716	2,880				
1920	3,054	23,619	854	10,829	1,000		2,000	
1895–1904		95,940	122,099	2,289	1,048	7,908		
1905–1914		76,929	18,226	25,406		19,316	1,977	
1915–1920	45,808	70,865	13,663	18,879	2,000	3,221	5,221	21
1895–1920	45,808	243,734	153,988	46,574	3,048	30,445	7,198	3

TABL

Year	Machinery b	Electrical Machinery	Transportation Equipment	Instruments	Miscellaneous Manufacturing	Total Manufacturing	Me Min
1895						6,270	
1896						2,691	
1897						4,421	4,6
1898	1,567	2,500		880		35,169	
1899			4,731		12,862	170,445	3,7
1900	5,585	2,000	10,420			42,223	
1901	2,510					129,411	2,5
1902	23,594	2,600	2,911	950	5,931	184,895	3,6
1903	4,920	1,880	718	4,800	1,977	78,821	12,2
1904	3,458	1,880	1,018		1,977	65,545	
1905	17,034		4,583			96,022	7,2
1906	10,916	2,301				102,380	45,4
1907	1,358		300		3,954	69,463	32,4
1908			700			18,410	
1909	680		10,132	1,500		44,897	2,5
1910	26,985		28,678			115,416	
1911	3,948				3,954	41,278	1,1
1912	3,880	3,760	16,052		1,977	124,687	
1913	8,154		4,813			102,939	
1914				880		94,980	3,6
1915	14,226	4,389	4,309			84,211	1,8
1916	5,326	1,553	20,415	6,442		251,004	
1917	10,652		29,703		669	253,259	1,4
1918		2,770	42,571			147,054	
1919	5,326	3,500	46,206		446	301,941	
1920	23,053	9,333	43,697	3,221	223	459,316	1,
1895–1904	41,634	10,860	19,798	6,630	22,747	719,891	26
1905–1914	72,955	6,061	65,558	2,380	9,885	810,472	92
1915–1920	58,583	21,545	186,901	9,663	1,338	1,496,785	6
1895–1920	173,172	38,466	272,257	18,673	33,970	3,027,148	125

b Except electrical.

ing	Chemicals	Petroleum, Coal	Rubber	Rubber	Stone, Glass	Primary Metals	Metal Products[a]	Year
						4,476		1895
	376							1896
		675						1897
	75	8,600				13,528		1898
	36,985	5,401				35,712		1899
	2,028		1,000		1,065	11,400		1900
	4,179				500	87,699	3,908	1901
	7,199				1,385	67,932	6,647	1902
	3,238				355	33,631	300	1903
77	564					41,618	829	1904
	1,912		5,401	4,531		32,574	2,368	1905
	4,233		7,520			41,972		1906
	3,000	955		1,015	710	47,901	2,361	1907
	1,688					8,976	1,829	1908
00			4,000		123	12,276		1909
	3,445	5,739			1,240	42,101	2,128	1910
	5,084					20,359	829	1911
	4,743		22,413	3,600		46,361	200	1912
	1,740	36,956	10,802	1,015		25,579	829	1913
77	788		5,401		300	75,092	829	1914
	19,285	1,339	1,430			21,154	1,913	1915
	5,741	84,129	2,710		7,500	90,845	4,916	1916
	24,622	52,302	3,010		150	69,476	7,865	1917
	20,607	7,945	1,430		3,750	38,858	12,796	1918
21	2,250	126,152	1,430		3,750	76,336	10,643	1919
	19,402	198,119	1,430	6,442	26,250	23,049	55,006	1920
77	54,644		14,676	1,000	3,305	295,996	11,684	1895–1904
77	26,633	43,650	55,537	10,161	2,373	353,191	11,373	1905–1914
21	91,907	469,986	11,440	6,442	41,400	319,718	93,139	1915–1920
75	173,184	513,636	81,653	17,603	47,078	968,905	116,196	1895–1920

xcept ordnance, machinery, and transportation epuipment.

inued

uminous Coal	Petroleum and Gas Extraction	Nonmetal Minerals[c]	Total Mining	Ice	Nonallocable	Total Manufacturing and Mining	Year
						6,270	1895
						2,691	1896
			4,630			9,051	1897
						35,169	1898
			3,780		3,540	177,765	1899
350	100		450	9,296	885	52,854	1900
2,208			24,708		2,655	156,774	1901
3,738			17,352		14,160	216,407	1902
7,688	303		70,201	1,328		150,350	1903
3,738		250	13,988			79,533	1904
9,202	3,100	650	40,171	1,328		137,521	1905
3,400	1,000		49,823	7,968	1,770	161,941	1906
7,244		2,650	42,357	5,312		117,132	1907
		650	650			19,060	1908
4,094		1,650	8,244			53,141	1909
4,064		1,142	25,206	1,328		141,950	1910
4,244	836		6,180	1,328		48,786	1911
8,232			8,232		885	133,804	1912
5,488			5,583		885	109,407	1913
			3,614			98,594	1914
			1,846			86,057	1915
7,980	552	1,626	11,008			258,791	1916
1,900	10,780	77	24,237		100	277,596	1917
4,480	5,460	8,000	47,940	5,000		199,994	1918
7,880	16,140	5,626	70,496	2,650	200	375,287	1919
4,920	34,278		70,973	2,950		533,239	1920
7,722	403	250	135,109	10,624	21,240	886,864	1895–1904
5,968	4,936	6,742	190,060	17,264	3,540	1,021,336	1905–1914
7,160	67,210	15,329	226,500	10,600	300	1,734,185	1915–1920
0,850	72,549	22,321	551,669	38,488	25,080	3,642,385	1895–1920

xcept fuels.

Year	Ordnance	Food	Tobacco	Textiles	Apparel	Lumber	Furniture	P
1895								
1896								
1897		3					1	
1898		7	3	1				
1899		21	1	7		1	1	
1900		7	1	1				
1901		5	2	2		1		
1902	1	7	2			1		
1903		1	1					
1904		4						
1905		5					1	
1906		1		1	1			
1907		3		3		1		
1908		1		3				
1909								
1910		3	1	1				
1911		1		1				
1912		1	1	1	1			
1913				1				
1914		2		1				
1915	1	2		1				
1916		2		2				
1917				1				
1918		1						
1919		5		2				
1920		1						
1895–1904	1	55	10	11		3	2	1
1905–1914		17	2	12	2	1	1	
1915–1920	1	11		6				
1895–1920	2	83	12	29	2	4	3	1

The figure for consolidation disappearances is net, e.g., when one company is formed by the uni̲
six companies, the net number of firm disappearances is five.

Year	Machinery[b]	Electrical Machinery	Transportation Equipment	Instruments	Miscellaneous Manufacturing	Total Manufacturing	Metal Minin
1895		1				4	
1896		2			1	5	
1897	1		1			9	
1898	1				1	23	
1899	7	1	9	3	1	96	3
1900	6	1	3	1		37	1
1901	6	1	1	2	1	36	3
1902	4				2	37	2
1903	3				1	14	1
1904						8	
1905	1	1	1			15	
1906						4	4
1907	1				1	11	
1908		2	1		1	9	1
1909	1		1			3	
1910			1			8	
1911	2		1		1	10	
1912	3		1	1		13	
1913						7	
1914						6	1
1915	1		3			12	
1916	1		7			19	
1917	1		1			19	
1918	2		1			5	1
1919	1	1	3			29	1
1920	1	1	3			15	
1895–1904	28	6	14	6	7	269	10
1905–1914	8	3	6	1	3	86	7
1915–1920	7	2	18			99	2
1895–1920	43	11	38	7	10	454	19

b Except electrical.

g	Chemicals	Petroleum, Coal	Rubber	Leather	Stone, Glass	Primary Metals	Metal Products[a]	Year
	1	1			1			1895
		1					1	1896
						3		1897
	2		1			4	1	1898
	5	1	2	1	4	22	5	1899
		1			5	4	4	1900
	4		1		4	3	3	1901
	1				1	11	4	1902
	1	1		1	1	2		1903
	1				1	1	1	1904
					1	2	2	1905
						1		1906
					1	1	1	1907
	1							1908
	1							1909
	1						1	1910
	1			1			1	1911
	1					3		1912
	1	1					4	1913
	1	1						1914
		1				3		1915
	1	2		1		3		1916
	5	4	1			2	2	1917
							1	1918
	1	6		1	2	4	3	1919
	2	2			2	2		1920
	15	5	4	2	17	50	19	1895–1904
	7	2		1	1	7	9	1905–1914
	9	15	1	2	4	14	6	1915–1920
	31	22	5	5	22	71	34	1895–1920

[a] ...ept ordnance, machinery, and transportation equipment.

...ued

minous oal	Petroleum and Gas Extraction	Nonmetal Minerals[c]	Total Mining	Ice	Nonallocable	Total Manufacturing and Mining	Year
				1		5	1895
						5	1896
						9	1897
				1		24	1898
2		2	7	1	1	105	1899
		4	5			42	1900
8		3	14	1		51	1901
5	1	1	9		1	47	1902
1			2			16	1903
1			1			9	1904
10		1	11	1		27	1905
4		1	9		1	14	1906
1			1			12	1907
		2	3			12	1908
		1	2			5	1909
5	2		7	1		16	1910
1	1		3	1	1	15	1911
						13	1912
		1	2	3		12	1913
						6	1914
				1		13	1915
				1		20	1916
2	1		4			23	1917
			1			6	1918
1	4	1	6			35	1919
1	1		2			17	1920
17	1	10	38	4	2	313	1895–1904
22	3	6	38	6	2	132	1905–1914
4	6	1	13	2		114	1915–1920
43	10	17	89	12	4	559	1895–1920

[c] ...ept fuels.

Year	Ordnance C	Ordnance A	Food C	Food A	Tobacco C	Tobacco A	Textiles C	Textiles A	Apparel C	Apparel A	Lumber C	Lumber A	Furniture C	Furniture A	… C
1895						5									
1896				2											
1897			36	3		1							2		
1898			101	8	11	3	13								33
1899			167	9	13	21	48				2		24		35
1900			28	8	2	6	1								3
1901			56	13	10	12	12	2			15				
1902	1		32	11	13	13					15	4			
1903			1	16	1	17		2		1					33
1904			25	8		5									4
1905			30	15		6		1					7		
1906			3	18		13	3	1	1					1	
1907			16	5			8	1			2				
1908			1	3			11								
1909				9				5							
1910			16	2	6		2	2				1			
1911			18	3			2	3							
1912			2	1	1	1	2	2	1			8			
1913				2		4	3	2							
1914			2	5			1	3							1
1915	2	3	7	2		2	2	4						1	
1916		2	7	5		2	3	3		1				1	
1917		6		16		3	1	7							
1918		2	1	7		2		1							7
1919		1	17	10		6	4	5				1			1
1920		1	1	10		1		7		1					
1895–1904	1		446	78	50	83	74	4		1	32	4	26		108
1905–1914			88	63	7	24	32	20	2		2	9	7	1	1
1915–1920	2	15	33	50		16	10	27		2		1		2	8
1895–1920	3	15	567	191	57	123	116	51	2	3	34	14	33	3	117

TABL

Year	Machinery[b] C	Machinery A	Electrical Machinery C	Electrical Machinery A	Transportation Equipment C	Transportation Equipment A	Instruments C	Instruments A	Miscellaneous Manufacturing C	Miscellaneous Manufacturing A	Total Manufacturing C	Total Manufacturing A	Metals/Mining C
1895			2								28	6	
1896			13								22	4	
1897	10				2				5		62	5	
1898	6	2		1				1	16		255	21	
1899	39		10		98	2	11		2	7	884	95	13
1900	19	3	4	1	11	6	1				268	38	1
1901	19	2	1		1		4		3		227	57	9
1902	9	15		1		4		1	20	3	197	88	10
1903	12	4		1		1		6	6	1	50	70	4
1904		2		1		2				1	30	38	
1905	1	10	1		1	6					57	63	
1906		8		2							8	62	10
1907	5	1				1			1	2	36	27	
1908				3	10	1			2		29	13	3
1909	1	1			1	8		1			10	32	
1910		19			9	8					41	57	
1911	11	6			1					2	39	28	1
1912	11	3		2	3	4	1			1	37	41	
1913		9				2					14	42	3
1914								1			19	19	
1915	2	5		4	3	1					26	39	
1916	1	2		1	19	6					42	63	
1917	4	4			3	9		2			62	97	7
1918	2			4	2	13				3	6	56	1
1919	1	2	2	2	5	8				2	62	76	
1920	3	9	2	5	6	13		1		1	42	133	
1895–1904	114	28	30	5	112	15	16	8	52	12	2,023	422	37
1905–1914	29	57	4	4	25	30	1	2	4	5	290	384	17
1915–1920	13	22	4	16	38	50		3		6	240	464	8
1895–1920	156	107	38	25	175	95	17	13	56	23	2,553	1,270	62

b Except electrical.

Chemicals		Petroleum, Coal		Rubber		Leather		Stone, Glass		Primary Metals		Metal Products[a]		Year
C	A	C	A	C	A	C	A	C	A	C	A	C	A	
9		13						4				1		1895
	2	2										2		1896
				1						12				1897
22	1			2	1					47	4	4		1898
82	44	12		8	1	21		41		239	8	32		1899
	4	6					1	109	3	46	5	35		1900
7	6			2				13	1	15	16	69	4	1901
1	11							10	3	33	13	28	8	1902
18	10					1		2	1	4	9		1	1903
1	3							2		1	12	1	1	1904
	7			1		4		2		3	11	6	2	1905
	6			3						1	8			1906
	1		2	2		1		2		3	5	1	3	1907
2	2										4		2	1908
8				1					1		5			1909
3	5		1						4		12	5	3	1910
2	6					1					7	1	1	1911
10	4			2		4				6	8		1	1912
3	1	2	7	2		1					11	6	1	1913
4	2	11		1					1		3		1	1914
	8	6	1	1						4	6		1	1915
	3	7	8	1	1				2	3	15		3	1916
24	11	16	11	3	1				1	2	17	3	3	1917
	8	8	1	1					1		7	1	5	1918
2	2	15	17	1		1		3	1	4	11	8	5	1919
5	9	6	25	1			2	12	7	6	7	7	22	1920
140	81	34		12	3	22	1	181	8	397	68	171	14	1895–1904
32	34	13	10		12	1	10	2	8	13	74	19	14	1905–1914
32	41	50	63	1	8	2	2	15	12	19	63	12	39	1915–1920
204	156	97	73	13	23	25	13	198	28	429	205	202	67	1895–1920

cept ordnance, machinery, and transportation equipment.

nued

	Petroleum and Gas Extraction		Nonmetal Minerals[c]		Total Mining		Ice		Nonallocable		Total Manufacturing and Mining		Year
minous Coal A	C	A	C	A	C	A	C	A	C	A	C	A	
							9				37	6	1895
											22	4	1896
						2					62	7	1897
							27				282	21	1898
			7		210	1	4		10	4	1,108	100	1899
1		1	23		24	2		7		1	292	48	1900
10			51		121	11	4		4	16	352	71	1901
6	37		5		67	7					268	111	1902
10			1	1	6	14		1			56	86	1903
4					6	5					36	43	1904
13			2	2	85	18	2	1			144	82	1905
2			5	1	35	12		6	3	2	46	82	1906
3			4		13	17		4			49	48	1907
			1		7	1					36	14	1908
2	7				2	5					12	37	1909
8	1	1			20	9	14	1			75	67	1910
3					10	5	12	1	8		69	34	1911
3						3				1	37	45	1912
2			4		7	4	18			1	39	46	1913
						4					19	20	1914
						2	4				30	41	1915
1		5		1	20	9	3				45	72	1916
3	4	5		1		15				1	82	113	1917
3		3	3		1	7		1			7	64	1918
6	8	8	2	2	12	18		1		2	74	97	1919
5	2	13			7	22		2			49	157	1920
31	37	2	86	1	434	42	44	8	14	20	2,515	497	1895–1904
36	8	4	16	9	179	74	46	13	11	4	526	475	1905–1914
18	14	34	2	5	40	73	7	4	7	3	287	544	1915–1920
85	59	40	104	15	653	189	97	25	25	32	3,328	1,516	1895–1920

cept fuels.

Appendix C
Tables Underlying Material Presented in the Text

TABLE C-1

100 Largest Manufacturing Corporations, 1955, Ranked by Asset Size and with Date of Most Important Merger, if Mergers Were Important in the Company's History

Rank	Name of Company	Date
1	Standard Oil (N.J.)	Pre-1895
2	General Motors	1908
3	U.S. Steel	1901
4	DuPont (E.I.) de Nemours	1895–1905
5	Ford Motor	None
6	Socony Mobiloil	Pre-1895
7	Standard Oil (Ind.)	Pre-1895
8	Gulf Oil	None
9	Texas Company	None
10	Bethlehem Steel	1902
11	Standard Oil (Calif.)	Pre-1895
12	General Electric	1901–1902
13	Union Carbide & Carbon	1917
14	Chrysler	1922
15	Westinghouse Electric	None
16	Western Electric	None
17	Sinclair Oil	None
18	Shell Oil	None
19	Phillips Petroleum	None
20	Cities Service	None
21	International Harvester	1902
22	Aluminum Co. of America	None
23	Anaconda	1899
24	American Tobacco	1895–1904
25	Kennecott Copper	None
26	Goodyear Tire & Rubber	None
27	Republic Steel	1899
28	Allied Chemical & Dye	1920
29	International Telephone & Telegraph	1949–1951
30	Dow Chemical	None
31	Radio Corp. of America	1929–1934
32	Jones & Laughlin Steel	None
33	Firestone Tire & Rubber	None
34	International Business Machines	1911
35	Olin Mathieson Chemical	1954
36	International Paper	1898
37	Reynolds (R.J.) Tobacco	1895–1904
38	Atlantic Refining	Pre-1895
39	Eastman Kodak	1903
40	National Steel	1929
41	U.S. Rubber	1893
42	Youngstown Sheet & Tube	1923
43	Armco Steel	None

TABLE C-1, continued

Rank	Name of Company	Date
44	Monsanto Chemical	None
45	Union Oil	1890
46	Swift	1900–1905
47	Sun Oil	None
48	Pittsburgh Plate Glass	1895
49	American Cyanamid	1929–1934
50	Inland Steel	None
51	Burlington Industries	1954
52	Goodrich (B.F.)	1912
53	Proctor & Gamble	None
54	Continental Oil	Pre-1895
55	Reynolds Metals	None
56	Tidewater Oil	1888
57	Sunray Mid-Continent Oil	1955
58	American Can	1901
59	Armour	None
60	National Dairy Products	1925–1930
61	Sperry Rand	1955
62	Liggett & Myers Tobacco	1895–1904
63	Pure Oil	1895
64	Deere	1911–1912
65	Allis-Chalmers Manufacturing	1901
66	Singer Manufacturing	1906
67	Phelps Dodge	None
68	Crown Zellerbach	1928
69	American Smelting & Refining	1899
70	Grace (W. R.)	1953–1954
71	National Distillers Products	1899
72	Seagram (Joseph E.) & Sons	None
73	Continental Can	1913
74	Schenley Industries	None
75	Weyerhaeuser Timber	None
76	General Foods	1929–1932
77	Kaiser Aluminum & Chemical	None
78	Ohio Oil	Pre-1895
79	Borg-Warner	1928–1929
80	National Lead	1906
81	Caterpillar Tractor	1925–1928
82	Standard Oil (Ohio)	Pre-1895
83	Celanese	None
84	Skelly Oil	None
85	Borden	1899–1904
86	Richfield Oil	None
87	Lockheed Aircraft	None
88	General Dynamics	1954
89	Stevens (J. P.)	None
90	Douglas Aircraft	None
91	Owens-Illinois Glass	1929
92	United Aircraft	1928
93	Wheeling Steel	1920
94	Bendix Aviation	1929

(concluded on next page)

TABLE C-1, concluded

Rank	Name of Company	Date
95	American Viscose	None
96	Kaiser Steel	None
97	Campbell Soup	1955
98	Philip Morris	None
99	North American Aviation	None
100	American Motors	1953

Sources: *The Fortune Magazine Directory of 500 Largest U.S. Industrial Corporations*, July 1956; data compiled in present study; basic data sheets for Fred J. Weston, *The Role of Mergers in the Growth of Large Firms*, University of California Press, 1953; Gertrude G. Schroeder, *The Growth of Major Steel Companies, 1900–1950*, Johns Hopkins Press, 1953; A. D. H. Kaplan, *Big Enterprise in a Competitive System*, Brookings, 1954; Moody's Manuals, 1929, 1939, and 1955.

TABLE C-2

Annual Rates of Production Growth for Forty-Four Production Series Relevant to the Industries of Highest 1895–1907 Merger Activity by Decades, 1870–1915

Industry and Production Series	Central Year of Decade							
	1875	1880	1885	1890	1895	1900	1905	1910
Food and Kindred Products:								
Cocoa imports	9.0	9.9	10.5	9.4	7.4	12.7	10.0	9.2
Coffee imports	3.9	5.8	1.8	2.3	5.1	3.6	0.4	0.3
Distilled spirits	1.5	3.4	0.9	2.9	−0.8	7.8	2.8	2.4
Fermented liquors	5.3	8.4	6.9	5.8	2.6	4.3	4.6	1.7
Raw sugar consumption	3.6	5.4	4.7	4.8	1.7	2.5	2.7	2.9
Flour	...	...	2.7	2.8	2.1	1.5	0.2	0.7
Canned corn	...	...	...	6.5	7.2	12.7	3.6	0.6
Canned tomatoes	...	...	...	7.9	4.3	7.1	5.3	4.0
Tobacco Products:								
Tobacco and snuff	3.3	5.5	5.0	3.0	1.3	3.6	3.3	1.7
Cigarettes	...	...	20.0	11.5	3.5	−0.6	11.5	16.5
Cigars	...	...	4.0	2.2	2.6	6.0	1.1	0.2
Tobacco consumption	...	...	3.5	2.3	1.1	4.2	3.3	1.8
Chemicals and Allied Products:								
Superphosphate	12.0	17.5	4.7	4.5	9.3	8.6	5.4	4.2
White lead	...	...	...	2.5	3.4	3.7	3.3	1.7
Phosphate rock	15.0	14.2 ·	8.7	10.2	10.0	6.7	6.5	3.9
Stone, Clay, and Glass Products:								
Fluorspar	...	...	9.7	4.5	6.9	23.0	7.2	12.7
Roofing slate	...	...	6.5	3.1	2.9	5.6	−0.8	−2.2
Cement, total	...	...	12.7	6.6	8.1	17.0	14.7	7.2
Gypsum	...	...	7.8	8.2	5.2	20.3	14.7	5.2
Portland cement	...	...	21.7	21.2	45.0	37.7	20.2	7.9

TABLE C-2, concluded

Industry and Production Series	Central Year of Decade							
	1875	1880	1885	1890	1895	1900	1905	1910
Iron and Steel Mills, Foundries, and Mines:								
Tin plate consumption	8.2	11.2	7.4	1.7	3.5	6.2	5.2	5.5
Iron ore	...	...	8.5	5.1	5.9	11.2	5.9	3.8
Pig iron	5.3	9.4	8.8	5.1	5.1	9.4	5.5	4.3
Rails	5.6	5.5	2.7	−1.3	4.3	9.3	1.3	−1.5
Steel	30.0	14.7	12.2	7.7	12.7	12.5	7.3	6.4
Rolled iron and steel	...	...	...	2.3	6.4	10.5	5.9	5.0
Transportation Equipment:								
Vessels	−4.1	−3.7	1.4	0.2	1.4	9.0	−2.3	−4.4
Locomotives	...	...	0.8	0.9	1.2	17.3	1.2	−4.3
Nonferrous Smelting, Refining, Mills, Foundries, and Mines:								
Copper Ore	7.8	17.2	14.2	9.7	8.7	7.1	6.5	4.3
Gold ore	−0.9	−2.7	−0.2	3.4	10.4	5.2	3.0	0.3
Lead, domestic	17.3	8.3	4.5	2.4	4.5	6.3	3.9	5.0
Silver	5.2	3.3	5.4	4.1	−0.4	0.0	−0.2	2.8
Zinc	14.2	11.0	8.8	7.2	6.2	9.0	7.8	7.5
Lead consumption	4.2	6.4	2.7	4.3	4.4	5.3	2.9	2.4
Lead, total	17.3	8.3	4.5	6.0	6.7	5.2	2.5	3.3
Tin imports	7.6	8.1	6.0	5.8	6.8	6.3	3.0	2.3
Zinc consumption	...	11.2	7.1	5.9	5.1	9.8	7.6	6.0
Gold consumption	...	...	5.4	1.5	0.7	10.3	5.1	2.5
Silver consumption	...	...	7.1	7.4	5.6	12.0	5.1	3.6
Aluminum	...	...	...	66.0	52.0	15.7	9.6	24.0
Copper consumption	...	...	...	8.2	6.6	10.3	4.8	5.4
Bituminous Coal Mining:								
Bituminous coal	5.4	12.5	6.5	5.8	6.1	9.6	6.1	4.0
Coal, total	5.1	10.4	6.0	5.3	4.9	8.2	5.7	3.6
Coke	...	...	11.5	6.2	6.6	9.4	6.4	3.5

Source: A. F. Burns, *Production Trends in The United States Since 1870*, National Bureau of Economic Research, 1934, pp. 306–308.

TABLE C-3

Merger Activity Classified by the Importance of Transportation Costs in the Delivered Price of the Product, 1895–1920

Market Size: L—Local R—Regional N—National	Code Durability: N—Nondurable S—Semidurable D—Durable	Stage of Fabrication: S—Semifinished F—Finished

| Industry | Net Firm Disappearances | | Market size | Durability | Fabrication |
	All mergers	Consolidations only			
Products with Local Markets:					
Crushed and broken stone (142)	26	26			
Cement (142)	8	8	R	D	S
Dimension stone (141)	21	21	R	D	F
Sand and gravel (144)	2	2			
Bakery products (205)	38	37	L	N	F
Bottled soft drinks (2081)	7	7	L	N	F
Malt liquors (2082)	95	91	R	N	F
Printing, publishing (27)	6	5	L–N	N	S–F
Bricks (3251)	49	48	R	D	F
Ice, natural and manufactured	52	44			
	304	289			
Products with National Markets and Low Transportation Costs Relative to Price:					
Confectionery and related products (27)	27	21	N	N	F
Wines (2084)	8	8	N	N	F
Distilled liquors (2085)	79	76	N	N	F
Tobacco products (21)	133	50	N	N	F
Apparel (23)	1	0	N	S	F
Industrial organic chemicals, mainly explosives (282)	48	4	N	N	F
Paints, varnishes, lacquers, etc. (285)	19	18	N	N	F
Rubber products (30)	15	12	N	S	F
Sandpaper (3291)	8	7	N	D	F
Metal products (34)	119	105	R–N	D	F
Machinery (except 36) (35)	142	114	N	D	F
Electrical machinery, etc. (36)	35	30	N	D	F
Transportation equipment (37)	127	112	N	D	F
Instruments (38)	24	16	N	D	F
	785	573			

TABLE C-3, concluded

Industry	Net Firm Disappearances		Market size	Dura- bility	Fabri- cation
	All mergers	Consoli- dations only			
Products with National Markets and High Transport Costs Relative to Price:					
Metal mining (10)	45	37			
Bituminous coal mining (12)	305	274	R	N	S–F
Petroleum and gas extraction (13)	39	37			
Meat products (201)	43	1	N	N	F
Grain mill products (204)	68	63	N	N	S
Sugar (206)	20	15	N	N	S–F
Malt (2083)	28	26	N	N	S
Lumber (24)	36	32	N	D	S
Furniture, fixtures (25)	26	26	N	D	F
Paper and allied products (26)	113	108	N	N	F
Fertilizers (287)	62	44	R	N	F
Petroleum products (29)	34	34	N	N	F
Flat glass (3211)	65	64	N	D	F
Clay sewer pipe (3254)	32	32	R	D	F
Clay refractories (3255)	10	10	R	D	F
Gypsum products (3272)	29	29	N	D	F
Asbestos products (3292)	2	0	N	D	F
Blast furnaces, steel works, rolling mills (331)	311	263	N	D	S
Iron and steel foundries (332)	79	74	R	D	S
Nonferrous smelting, refining, rolling mills and foundries (333–336)	44	33	N	D	S
Tin cans (341)	66	66	N	S	F
	1,457	1,258			
Non-allocable:					
Ordnance (19)	1	1			
Dairy products (202)	7	4	L–N	N	F
Canning and preserving fruits, vegetables and sea foods (203)	79	74	N	N	F
Textiles (22)	78	74	N	S	S
Chemicals and allied products not otherwise allocated (286, 288, 289)	104	60			
Leather and products (31)	23	22	N	S	S–F
Glassware (322)	41	41	N	D	F
Miscellaneous and not otherwise classified	133	97			
	466	373			

Sources: Disappearances data from worksheets and from Appendix B; classifications of products characteristics from *The Structure of American Industry*, National Resources Committee, Washington, D.C., 1939, Part I, Appendix 8, pp. 264–269.

TABLE C-4

Measures of Relative Merger Activity and Geographical Concentration, 1895–1920

Standard Industrial Classification	Ratio of Merger Capital to Total Industry Capital		Geographical Concentration	
	All mergers	Consolidations only	Three adjacent leading states	Index
201	0.295	0.013	Ill., Mo., Kan.	0.547
202	.201	.138	Wis., Iowa, Ill.	.334
203	.786	.728	Md., N.J., N.Y.	.347
204	.153	.138	Minn., Ill., Wis.	.274
21	.949	.573	N.Y., Pa., Ohio	.543
22	.136	.135	Mass., N.Y., Pa.	.480
24, 25	.083	.068	Minn., Mich., Wis.	.180
26	.561	.541	Pa., N.Y., Mass.	.455
27	.031	.026	N.Y., Pa., Ohio	.336
282	.061	.041	Pa., Ohio., Ind.	.280
285	.334	.324	N.Y., Pa., Ohio	.542
287	.953	.746	Ga., N.C., S.C.	.274
291	.007	.007	Del., Pa.	.365
311	.163	.159	Pa., N.Y., Mass.	.505
321–323	.402	.398	Pa., Ind., Ohio	.636
3211	...	...	Pa., Ind., Ohio	.801
3251	...	...	N.Y., Pa., Ohio	.288
3254	...	...	Ohio, Ind., Pa.	.476
3255	...	...	Ohio, Pa., Ky.	.709
331, 332	2.505	2.311	Pa., Ohio, N.J.	.688
3333	...	...	Ill., Mo., Kan.	.691
352	.730	.709	Ill., Ind., Ohio	.518
36	.439	.388	N.Y., Mass., Pa.	.571
371	2.190	1.654	Ohio, Mich., Ind.	.507
373	.342	.328	Pa., N.Y., N.J.	.348

Source: Worksheets of Appendix B, *Census of Manufacturers, 1905, op. cit.*

TABLE C-5
Mergers Achieving Market Dominance, 1895–1904

Company	Net Firm Disappearances	Capitalization (millions of dollars)	Percentage of Market Controlled
42.5%–62.5%:			
Allis Chalmers	3	50.0	50
American Felt	4	5.0	60
American Shipbuilding	7	30.0	60
American Stove	8	5.0	60
American Writing Paper	27	25.0	55
Asphalt Co. of America	12	30.0	35–50
Computing Scale	2	3.5	50
Distilling Co. of America	73	125.0	60
International Paper	24	45.0	60
International Salt	27	30.0	30–60
National Candy	13	9.0	55
National Enameling & Stamping	9	30.0	55
National Glass	18	3.0	50–70
Royal Baking Powder	4	20.0	58–65
Rubber Goods Manufacturing	6	50.0	40–60
Standard Table Oil Cloth	6	10.0	50
United Button	2	3.0	45
U.S. Cotton Duck	12	50.0	45–65
U.S. Envelope	9	5.0	50–60
U.S. Shipbuilding	8	45.0	40–60
Virginia-Carolina Chemical	15	10.0	60
62.5%–82.5%:			
American Can	64	88.0	65–75
American Car & Foundry	12	60.0	65
American Fork & Hoe	12	4.0	80
American Hide & Leather	21	35.0	75
American Locomotive	8	50.0	70
American Radiator	3	10.0	80
American School Furniture	24	10.0	80
American Sugar Refining	6	145.0	70–90
California Fruit Canners	9	3.5	65
Casein Co. of America	4	6.5	70
Central Foundry	30	14.0	80
Chicago Pneumatic Tool	4	7.5	80
Federal Publishing	3	6.0	75
General Chemical	15	25.0	70
Harbison-Walker Refractories	10	27.6	70
International Harvester	4	120.0	70
International Steam Pump	4	27.5	80
National Biscuit	27	55.0	70
National Fireproofing	22	15.5	65
National Novelty	19	10.0	70
Otis Elevator	6	11.0	65
Standard Sanitary	8	5.0	80
Union Bag & Paper	5	27.5	80
U.S. Gypsum	29	7.5	80
U.S. Steel	170	1,370.0	65

(concluded on next page)

TABLE C-5, concluded

Company	Net Firm Disappearances	Capitalization (millions of dollars)	Percentage of Market Controlled
82.5% and over:			
American Brake Shoe & Foundry	4	4.5	90
American Caramel	1	1.5	90
American Chicle	5	9.0	85
American Grass Twine	3	15.0	90
American Linseed	6	33.5	85
American Pneumatic Service	2	15.0	87
American Seeding Machine	7	15.0	90
American Smelting & Refining	12	65.0	85
American Tobacco	162	502.0	90
Diamond Match	38	19.5	85
DuPont (E.I.) de Nemours	65	50.0	85
General Electric & Westinghouse	8	162.0	90
National Carbon	10	10.0	87
Pullman	1	74.0	85
Railway Steel Spring	7	20.0	95
U.S. Bobbin & Shuttle	4	2.0	90
"Large":			
American Agricultural Chemical	32	40.0	
American Sewer Pipe	6	10.0	
Borden	6	20.0	
Brewery Consolidations (12)	97	67.1	
Corn Products Refining	3	80.0	
Ice Consolidations (4)	61	74.4	
International Nickel	3	24.0	
International Silver	16	20.0	
National Lead	18	25.0	
United Shoe Machinery	3	20.0	

Source: Disappearance and capitalizations data from worksheets; data on percentage of market controlled from John Moody, *The Truth about the Trusts*, Moody, 1904.

TABLE C-6

Early Consolidations that Appeared in Subsequent Larger Mergers

Consolidations later Entering	Year of Earlier Consolidations	Number of Firms Acquired	Capitalization (millions of dollars)
U.S. Steel (1901):			
Shelby Steel Tube	1897	5	5.0
American Steel & Wire (Ill.)	1898	6	24.0
Federal Steel	1898	6	200.0
American Tin Plate	1898	35	50.0
American Steel & Wire (N.J.)	1899	28	90.0
American Steel Hoop	1899	11	33.0
National Steel	1899	8	59.0
National Tube	1899	17	80.0
American Bridge	1900	27	70.0
American Sheet Steel	1900	26	52.0
Distilling Co. of America (1899):			
Standard Distilling and Distributing	1898	11	24.0
Kentucky Distilleries & Warehouse	1899	56	32.0
Corn Products (1902):			
Glucose Sugar Refining	1897	6	40.0
National Starch	1900	4	9.5
American Tobacco (1903):			
Atlantic Snuff	1898	4	10.0
Continental Tobacco	1898	8	75.0
Union Tobacco	1898	2	10.0
Havana-Commercial	1899	14	20.0
Havana-American	1899	8	10.0
American Snuff	1900	3	25.0
American Cigar	1901	9	10.0
Westinghouse:			
Walker	1896	3	2.5
U.S. Cotton Duck (1901):			
Mount Vernon-Woodberry	1899	7	9.5
International Salt (1901):			
National Salt	1899	26	12.0

Source: Moody, *The Truth About the Trusts.*

TABLE C-7

Quarterly Series of Firm Disappearances by Merger, Industrial Stock Prices, and Industrial Production, 1895–1955

Year and Quarter		Disappearances		Stock Prices	Industrial Production (1947–49 = 100)
		Original data	Seasonally adjusted data		
1895	1	3	3	35.5	13.8
	2	14	9	42.0	13.8
	3	24	27	41.8	14.7
	4	1	4	37.3	14.8
1896	1	3	2	35.5	14.0
	2	7	5	36.1	13.3
	3	0	0	28.7	12.9
	4	1	3	35.3	13.1
1897	1	8	6	31.1	13.8
	2	0	0	30.5	14.4
	3	38	45	38.0	15.8
	4	17	42	37.0	16.5
1898	1	132	89	35.7	16.3
	2	64	58	37.2	16.3
	3	19	23	42.3	16.0
	4	76	146	42.6	16.6
1899	1	410	273	49.8	17.2
	2	271	272	54.8	17.7
	3	316	389	55.9	18.5
	4	128	195	54.1	18.6
1900	1	147	103	49.2	18.6
	2	55	60	45.1	18.7
	3	60	69	43.1	17.4
	4	53	70	47.6	17.4
1901	1	97	72	51.7	19.0
	2	120	131	56.0	20.0
	3	61	68	54.1	20.3
	4	112	136	48.8	20.2
1902	1	113	88	49.2	20.5
	2	57	61	49.9	20.8
	3	96	103	49.8	21.2
	4	67	81	47.6	22.4
1903	1	45	36	49.4	22.8
	2	22	22	46.2	23.1
	3	35	39	38.7	23.0
	4	14	17	34.2	20.7
1904	1	27	22	36.4	21.4
	2	15	14	36.8	22.5
	3	4	4	40.6	21.7
	4	17	23	50.0	23.5
1905	1	55	45	55.9	24.6
	2	61	53	57.9	25.8
	3	60	70	60.9	26.0
	4	23	32	65.7	26.2

TABLE C-7, continued

Year and Quarter		Disappearances		Stock Prices	Industrial Production (1947-49=100)
		Original data	Seasonally adjusted data		
1906	1	22	19	73.5	27.1
	2	41	33	69.2	25.8
	3	13	16	69.9	26.3
	4	22	31	71.4	26.8
1907	1	44	41	67.5	27.9
	2	20	15	61.3	29.1
	3	16	20	56.8	28.4
	4	5	7	44.8	25.0
1908	1	5	5	47.5	22.5
	2	9	7	54.0	21.8
	3	11	13	60.6	23.5
	4	16	22	63.7	25.4
1909	1	4	4	63.7	26.1
	2	13	9	67.8	27.0
	3	6	8	73.3	28.7
	4	16	21	74.2	29.9
1910	1	62	68	69.2	30.2
	2	36	23	65.6	29.8
	3	22	31	59.3	28.7
	4	14	19	62.5	28.5
1911	1	9	9	63.4	28.0
	2	47	30	63.9	28.4
	3	14	21	61.7	28.6
	4	24	32	59.8	28.8
1912	1	20	20	62.4	30.5
	2	31	20	67.6	30.5
	3	12	20	68.8	31.5
	4	13	17	68.3	33.3
1913	1	28	28	62.1	33.4
	2	28	18	59.1	33.6
	3	5	9	60.3	33.1
	4	7	9	58.8	32.0
1914	1	20	21	61.8	31.1
	2	3	2	60.7	30.4
	3	5	8	57.9	30.3
	4	7	8	55.0	28.7
1915	1	4	4	57.0	29.9
	2	22	15	66.9	31.7
	3	8	12	78.9	33.8
	4	28	32	94.6	37.0
1916	1	13	15	93.8	38.3
	2	46	33	90.2	37.0
	3	16	21	92.3	37.3
	4	32	36	102.8	39.0
1917	1	55	64	94.2	40.4
	2	36	27	94.7	42.6
	3	46	53	88.4	40.1
	4	37	42	73.6	40.2

TABLE C-7, continued

Year and Quarter		Disappearances			Stock Prices	Industrial Production (1947–49=100)
		Original data		Seasonally adjusted data		
1918	1	19		21		78.2	38.4
	2	17		13		79.7	41.5
	3	14		15		82.1	40.6
	4	11		13		84.2	37.1
1919	1	19	57	20	51	83.6	37
	2	50	82	41	91	98.0	37
	3	56	147	56	144	107.0	41
	4	38	125	47	131	110.4	40
1920	1	78	209	74	186	100.1	44
	2	48	186	41	210	94.1	42
	3	28	188	27	192	87.5	41
	4	42	166	55	165	78.8	36
1921	1		184		162	75.2	31
	2		99		114	74.3	30
	3		80		84	68.3	31
	4		122		116	75.7	33
1922	1		86		74	83.8	35
	2		53		62	92.9	38
	3		82		90	97.6	40
	4		76		70	97.5	45
1923	1		84		71	101.0	47
	2		67		77	96.2	49
	3		44		49	90.2	48
	4		105		99	91.0	46
1924	1		110		94	97.4	46
	2		71		78	91.9	43
	3		87		97	101.9	42
	4		85		83	108.2	45
1925	1		124		108	120.8	48
	2		104		106	124.7	48
	3		127		140	138.4	48
	4		175		181	153.0	50
1926	1		286		258	152.9	50
	2		236		223	143.0	51
	3		171		186	160.5	52
	4		146		159	155.3	52
1927	1		161		152	157.6	52
	2		247		220	167.2	52
	3		220		236	184.8	51
	4		213		242	192.6	50
1928	1		197		196	199.6	51
	2		315		268	213.4	52
	3		242		259	225.8	54
	4		274		311	267.0	57
1929	1		349		369	308.4	58
	2		395		324	312.0	60
	3		312		337	354.3	61
	4		160		177	255.6	56

166

TABLE C-7, continued

Year and Quarter	Disappearances		Stock Prices	Industrial Production (1947–49=100
	Original data	Seasonally adjusted data		
1930 1	204	230	267.1	54
2	237	188	265.1	51
3	156	165	227.9	47
4	189	208	184.0	44
1931 1	163	194	176.3	42
2	142	111	146.2	43
3	87	89	134.5	40
4	71	79	94.8	36
1932 1	7	8	79.5	34
2	102	80	54.2	30
3	46	44	61.0	29
4	40	46	62.1	32
1933 1	19	22	58.2	30
2	43	35	81.3	37
3	33	31	99.0	44
4	12	14	95.4	38
1934 1	19	21	104.0	40
2	25	22	98.6	43
3	34	30	91.4	38
4	23	27	97.7	39
1935 1	36	36	102.3	45
2	27	26	111.2	44
3	38	35	126.8	47
4	24	27	140.4	51
1936 1	39	36	151.0	50
2	25	27	152.4	54
3	27	26	164.9	57
4	32	34	177.6	61
1937 1	32	30	185.9	63
2	27	30	173.3	65
3	29	30	173.7	64
4	31	30	129.7	52
1938 1	32	31	122.5	45
2	20	22	115.8	44
3	22	24	139.1	48
4	33	29	150.7	53
1939 1	24	24	144.2	54
2	22	24	131.7	54
3	16	18	140.1	59
4	25	21	150.0	66
1940 1	29	31	147.6	63
2	45	49	132.6	63
3	30	34	126.8	67
4	36	29	132.4	73
1941 1	22	25	124.1	79
2	23	26	118.9	85
3	24	27	126.9	89
4	42	32	117.0	93

TABLE C-7, continued

Year and Quarter		Disappearances		Stock Prices	Industrial Production (1947–49= 100)
		Original data	Seasonally adjusted data		
1942	1	19	22	107.5	98
	2	17	19	100.0	102
	3	31	34	106.6	108
	4	51	38	115.1	117
1943	1	44	50	127.6	123
	2	43	50	138.1	127
	3	47	51	138.8	129
	4	79	59	135.3	130
1944	1	68	78	137.3	129
	2	73	85	140.6	126
	3	79	84	146.7	123
	4	104	78	148.0	123
1945	1	59	68	155.9	125
	2	53	60	164.3	119
	3	79	84	169.9	100
	4	142	109	188.9	87
1946	1	95	108	196.4	85
	2	132	146	205.4	87
	3	109	114	190.5	93
	4	83	65	170.5	96
1947	1	98	112	178.1	99
	2	97	104	171.2	99
	3	84	87	180.5	99
	4	125	102	180.5	102
1948	1	60	67	172.6	103
	2	55	59	185.6	103
	3	52	53	182.8	104
	4	52	44	180.4	104
1949	1	31	34	176.7	99
	2	26	28	170.9	95
	3	31	31	177.5	96
	4	33	29	191.2	96
1950	1	46	51	203.2	100
	2	58	61	217.7	109
	3	51	51	215.0	118
	4	64	57	229.3	121
1951	1	46	50	249.1	122
	2	43	45	252.3	122
	3	66	67	264.0	118
	4	72	63	265.1	119
1952	1	69	76	267.1	121
	2	69	72	264.2	119
	3	74	77	275.0	122
	4	76	66	276.7	132
1953	1	55	60	286.4	134
	2	87	90	273.0	136
	3	55	59	268.1	135
	4	91	77	276.3	129

TABLE C-7, concluded

Year and Quarter	Disappearances		Stock Price	Industrial Production (1947–49 = 100)
	Original data	Seasonally adjusted data		
1954 1	74	82	292.6	124
2	72	74	320.6	124
3	109	119	346.7	123
4	130	108	376.0	128
1955 1			405.9	133
2			428.4	138
3			465.3	140
4			471.3	143

Sources: *Mergers*: For the sources of the series on firm disappearances by merger see Chapter 2, Table 2, of this monograph. The merger turning points were dated by the business cycle staff of the National Bureau of Economic Research. The merger series was deseasonalized in the UNIVAC program, and the deseasonalized series was used in dating the turning points.

Stock Prices: The quarterly index of stock prices from 1897 through 1955 was derived from the Dow-Jones monthly index of stock prices by taking the arithmetic mean of the three monthly indexes for a given quarter. The continuity of the index was broken in December 1914, when the number of stocks was increased from 12 to 20. The two series were spliced as of this date, the pre-1914 indexes being multiplied by the ratio (0.756) of the new to the old index for the period of overlap. The index for 1895–1896 was derived from A. M. Mathews, "New York Bank Clearings and Stock Prices, 1866–1914," *Review of Economics and Statistics*, October 1926, p. 193, Chart 7. The data, seasonally adjusted, were obtained from the National Bureau's business cycle files.

Industrial Production: The quarterly series of industrial production for the years 1895–1918 was derived from the Babson monthly index of business activity by taking the arithmetic mean of the three monthly indexes of a given quarter. This was spliced to the Federal Reserve Board Index, using the ratio (0.508) for the year 1919, to provide a continuous series from 1895 to 1955. The pre-1919 seasonally adjusted data were obtained from National Bureau's business cycle files. The Federal Reserve series, seasonally adjusted, was taken from the *Federal Reserve Bulletin*.

Appendix D. Absolute and Relative Measures of Merger Activity

The distribution of absolute merger activity among industries is influenced by their different sizes. Whether one industry is larger than another by virtue of having more firms of the same size, or the same number of firms of larger size, or a combination of the two, we should expect, other things being equal, to find higher firm disappearances or disappearance capitalizations (or both) in the larger industry.

To remove the effect of varying industry size, merger activity will be expressed as a percentage of industry size. Thus the industrial composition of merger activity can be described in terms of the importance to the industry of its merger activity. A classification based on relative merger activity is more meaningful for making inter-industry comparisons and for analysis of the causes of the merger movement.

The measures of industry size are taken from the special industry studies volume of the 1904 Census of Manufactures, which present capital and number-of-establishments data for forty industries or product groups. Direct comparison of merger activity to industry size, for these two measures of size, was possible for twenty-five of the forty industries at (with seven exceptions) a three-digit industry level of detail. The industries included in the comparisons were found in fifteen of the twenty-one two-digit manufacturing industries categories.[1]

The ratios so computed are subject to a substantial range of error and do not permit measurement of the relative amount of merger activity industry by industry. They are useful, nevertheless, as a basis for an approximate ranking of industries according to degree of merger activity.[2]

[1] The omission of six two-digit industries from the relative size measures probably does not affect the comparison of absolute to relative merger activity very much. Of these six two-digit industries, four (19, 23, 30, 38) exhibited very little absolute merger activity, having only sixty (gross) disappearances among them. One category (39) is a miscellaneous catch-all category; and fabricated metal products (34) had high absolute merger activity with 219 (gross) disappearances.

[2] The merger capital data are not directly comparable to the industry capital data. The census industry capital data were obtained from survey questionnaires sent to manufacturing establishments. Respondents were asked to list the value of their land, plant and equipment, and working capital. The capital thus reported would probably correspond to the balance sheet item "gross assets." The merger capital data gathered in this study, on the other hand, was that of the authorized stock capitalization of the corporations, and it was not possible to break down capitalization into issued and unissued stock. Add to this the incompleteness of reporting acknowledged in the census report, and the varying

170

The two ratios of merger activity to industry size are presented in Table D-1, where the fourteen included industries are also ranked by relative amount of merger activity. The two lists agree fairly closely on the industries of highest relative merger activity. Six industries—primary metals, transportation equipment, machinery (except electrical), paper and allied products, chemicals, and

TABLE D-1

Ratio of 1895–1907 Merger Activity to 1904 Industry Size for
Fourteen Two-Digit Manufacturing Industries

Industry	Merger Capital as Percentage of Industry Capital		Merger Disappearance as Percentage of Industry Establishments	
	Percentage	Rank	Percentage	Rank
Primary metals (33)	210.0	1	67.16	1
Transportation equipment (37)	75.1	2	30.43	2
Machinery (except 36) (35)	71.9	3	6.94	7
Paper and allied products (26)	56.7	4	16.69	4
Chemicals (28)	50.6	5	8.48	6
Tobacco products (21)	47.6	6	24.15	3
Electrical machinery, etc. (36)	43.8	7	5.36	8
Stone, clay, glass products (32)	40.8	8	3.27	9
Food and kindred products (20)	39.4	9	1.12	12
Leather and products (31)	18.6	10	2.86	10
Textiles (22)	14.5	11	2.24	11
Lumber, wood products (24) and furniture, fixtures (25)	8.2	12	0.41	13
Printing, publishing (27)	4.9	13	0.06	14
Petroleum products (29)	1.5	14	16.33	5

Source: Tables of this study and *Census of Manufactures, 1905*, Vols. III and IV.

amounts of "watered assets" and "watered stock" in both the census and the present compilations, and the comparability of the two sets of data is seen to be limited.

The lack of complete comparability between industry and merger capital does not exclude the possibility of making an interindustry comparison of some value, however. It does not seem unwarranted to assume that the biases in both the census and the data on merger activity are common to all industries in roughly similar degree. While the ratios do not indicate, even approximately, the actual degree of merger activity in a given industry, they do permit a rough ranking of industries in order of relative merger activity.

The data on firm disappearances compiled in this study are also not directly comparable to the data on number of manufacturing establishments in the census reports. This is because many firms consist of more than one establishment. Moreover, neither establishment nor firm-disappearance data take account of the sizes of firms or establishments. To justify making interindustry comparisons of ratios of merging firms to total industry establishments would require some drastic assumptions: first, that the proportions of firms of given numbers of plants are the same in the merging-firm group as in the firm population of the industry; second, that the merging firms are representative, as well, in terms of plant size. In view of the wide variations among industries in the number and proportion of small single-establishment firms and large multi-establishment firms, these assumptions are truly extreme. However, a comparison of the ratios of firm disappearances to total industry establishments will permit at least a rough ranking by industry of relative merger activity, and will serve as a check on the ranking made by use of capital data.

tobacco products—are among the seven most active industries in both lists. The coefficient of rank correlation between the two measures of relative merger activity is +0.736, further indicating a reasonably high correspondence between the rankings of the two lists.

Comparison of Absolute and Relative Measures of Merger Activity

The industries with the highest absolute merger activity usually also had the highest relative merger activity. This is demonstrated in Tables D-2 and D-3. Table D-2 compares the absolute and rela-

TABLE D-2

Absolute and Relative Merger Activity Measured by Capital, 1895–1907
(*merger capitalizations in thousands of dollars*)

Industry	Absolute Merger Activity		Relative Merger Activity	
	Adjusted merger capitalizations	Rank	Percentage	Rank
Primary metals (33)	3,168.4	1	210.0	1
Food and kindred products (20)	937.8	2	39.4	9
Machinery (except 36) (35)	404.0	3	71.9	3
Transportation equipment (37)	391.0	4	75.1	2
Tobacco products (21)	314.3	5	47.6	6
Chemicals (28)	245.3	6	50.6	5
Textiles (22)	213.5	7	14.5	11
Stone, clay, glass products (32)	160.5	8	40.5	8
Paper and allied products (26)	157.4	9	56.7	4
Electrical machinery, etc. (36)	78.8	10	43.8	7
Petroleum products (29)	74.0	11	1.5	14
Leather and products (31)	45.2	12	18.6	10
Lumber, wood products (24) and furniture, fixtures (25)	42.3	13	8.2	12
Printing, publishing (27)	18.9	14	4.9	13

Sources: Tables B-3 and D-1.

tive merger activity, as measured by capital in the fourteen industries for which comparisons were possible. The coefficient of rank correlation is +0.736,[3] indicating a fairly high correspondence between absolute and relative merger activity. Five industries—primary metals, machinery (except electrical), transportation equipment, tobacco products, and chemicals and allied products—are found in the six most active industries in both groups of fourteen.

A somewhat lower degree of correspondence between absolute and relative merger activity is found if the firm disappearance—

[3] This is coincidentally the same as the rank correlation between the two measures of relative merger activity.

establishments ratio is used to express relative merger activity. The comparison of absolute numbers of firm disappearances with the relative measures of firm disappearances is presented in Table D-3.

TABLE D-3

Absolute and Relative Merger Activity Measured by Firm Disappearances, 1895–1907

Industry	Absolute Merger Activity		Relative Merger Activity	
	Firm disappearances	Rank	Percentage	Rank
Food and kindred products (20)	671	1	1.12	12
Primary metals (33)	554	2	67.16	1
Chemicals (28)	252	3	8.48	6
Stone, clay, glass products (32)	211	4	3.27	9
Machinery (except 36) (35)	192	5	6.94	7
Tobacco products (21)	172	6	24.15	3
Transportation equipment (37)	153	7	30.43	2
Paper and allied products (26)	127	8	16.69	4
Textiles (22)	106	9	2.24	11
Lumber, wood products (24) and furniture, fixtures (25)	79	10	0.41	14
Electrical machinery, etc. (36)	42	11	5.36	8
Petroleum products (29)	41	12	16.33	5
Leather and products (31)	30	13	2.86	10
Printing, publishing (27)	15	14	0.06	14

Source: Tables B-7 and D-1.

The coefficient of rank correlation between absolute and relative activity in this case is $+0.363$, only a moderate correspondence. However, five industries—the same five just described—are found among the seven most active industries in both groups of fourteen.

Whether measured in relative or in absolute terms, the leading industries in merger activity seem to be primary metals, machinery (except electrical), transportation equipment, tobacco products, and chemicals and allied products. One other industry, food and kindred products, may belong among the leaders. In absolute merger activity it ranks first in disappearances and second in capitalizations. Its low ranking in the relative listings probably derives from two factors. First, sectors described in the industry studies of the 1904 Census accounted for only two-fifths of food products merger activity; the major share of merger activity lay outside the comparison. Second, the sectors of the industry entering into the comparison were characterized by many small establishments and many multiplant firms (meat packing, canning and preserving, dairy products, and grain mill products). In such industries we would expect considerable understatement in relative merger activity when using these measures.

Index

175

HOW TO OBTAIN NATIONAL BUREAU PUBLICATIONS

NATIONAL BUREAU BOOKS are available from bookstores or Princeton University Press, Princeton, New Jersey, except that contributors and subscribers to the National Bureau should order directly from the Bureau. OCCASIONAL and TECHNICAL PAPERS, EXPLORATORY REPORTS, and ANNUAL REPORTS are available from the National Bureau of Economic Research, 261 Madison Avenue, New York 16, New York.

SOME PUBLICATIONS OF THE
NATIONAL BUREAU OF ECONOMIC RESEARCH

BOOKS

Business Incorporations in the United States, 1800–1943 1948 192 pp. $6.00
George Heberton Evans, Jr.

Concentration in the Canadian Manufacturing Industries 1957 168 pp. $3.50
Gideon Rosenbluth

Corporate Cash Balances 1914–43: Manufacturing and Trade 1945 148 pp. $2.00
Frederick A. Lutz

The Volume of Corporate Bond Financing since 1900 1953 464 pp. $7.50
W. Braddock Hickman

Business Concentration and Price Policy, Special Conference, Series 5 1955 524 pp. $9.00

Corporate Income Retention, 1915–43 1951 142 pp. $2.50
Sergei P. Dobrovolsky

Conference on Research in Business Finance, Special Conference, Series 3 1952 360 pp. $5.00

Cost Behavior and Price Policy 1943 376 pp. $3.00
Commitee on Price Determination

The Trend of Government Activity in the United States since 1900 1952 288 pp. $4.00
Solomon Fabricant

The Frontiers of Economic Knowledge 1954 375 pp. $5.00
Arthur F. Burns

OCCASIONAL PAPERS

Trends and Cycles in Capital Formation by United States Railroads, 1870–1950 1954 $1.50
Melville J. Ulmer

Electronic Computers and Business Indicators 1957 $0.75
Julius Shiskin

Measuring Recessions 1958 $1.00
Geoffrey H. Moore